"In *Reparenting Your Inner Child*, the author skillfully guides readers to heal childhood wounds by cultivating self-compassion and resilience. Through heartfelt insights and practical strategies, this transformative journey helps you reclaim authenticity and form healthier patterns in daily life. Each chapter delivers empathy, understanding, and empowerment, making it a go-to resource for anyone eager to break free from old narratives. I endorse it as a beacon of hope and healing."

—**Sherrie Campbell, PhD**, psychologist, TEDx speaker, social media influencer, and author of *Adult Survivors of Toxic Family Members*

"What I like most about this book is the voice of the author. It is patient, loving, and encouraging; thus, a great model for reparenting both your present-day self and your wounded child parts. The relevant conceptual frameworks, illustrative stories, and exercises provide scaffolding for healing childhood wounds through the powerful tool of reparenting."

—**Jasmin Lee Cori, MS**, author of *The Emotionally Absent Mother*; and the workbook, *Healing from an Emotionally Absent Mother*

"Nicole's book on reparenting your inner child is a transformative guide for healing trauma. With her extensive education and expertise, she presents complex psychological concepts in clear, relatable language. This compassionate and empathetic work is accessible to all, providing solid evidence and practical advice. An invaluable resource, Nicole's book is a beacon of hope and understanding, destined to change lives."

—**Rebecca Gonzales, LMFT-S, LCPC-S, CFTP**, psychotherapist, and owner of Cornerstone Family Therapy

"It's no surprise to me that one of the most authentic, knowledgeable, and dedicated people I've ever met has written a generationally important book. I say this with full confidence: anyone who applies the teachings of *Reparenting Your Inner Child* in honest and full spirit will be rewarded with transformational healing and growth."

—**Will Watson**, cofounder of the Academy of Self Help, and author of *As Far As I Can Tell*

"Not only is Nicole professionally knowledgeable about the topic of trauma and reparenting the inner child, she speaks from the heart, having a true passion for the topic and to see people improve their lives. *Reparenting Your Inner Child* is truly a labor of love for Nicole, and it shows. This is a great companion guide for my therapy clients as they begin to recognize and address their childhood trauma."

—Sara Lupardus, LCSW, owner of Enlightened Therapy Solutions, ADHD-Certified Clinical Services Professional, and neurodivergent-focused diagnostician/clinician with a focus on complex trauma

"Nicole Johnson gives a voice to the inner child whose unmet needs can now be satisfied. She takes readers through the reparenting process to strengthen one's sense of self, and promote both self-awareness and self-compassion. The book is a digestible read with thought-provoking prompts for healing."

—Jamie Lewis, PhD, clinical child psychologist in Austin, TX

"Inner child work can be daunting. But Nicole Johnson masterfully breaks down the process—from understanding what happened and how it impacted you, to practical strategies and exercises to help you heal. If you didn't get the parenting you needed as a child, *Reparenting Your Inner Child* can show you how to gently and compassionately give your adult self and your wounded inner children the love you all deserve."

—Krylyn Peters, LPC, psychotherapist, educator, consultant, and founder of the Adult Children of Narcissists Conference (ACONcon)

"The first breath of Nicole Johnson in *Reparenting Your Inner Child* is compassionate and relieving. Her words are a salve for hurting souls and a gentle guide to finding, comforting, and healing our long-ignored childhood wounds. Johnson's approach to freedom from trauma is tender, approachable, and filled with the empathy many of us have longed for. Find a cozy spot, curl up with a copy, and get to work."

—Mary Mathis Burnett, EdD, instructor and inclusive pedagogy specialist at Arizona State University

Reparenting Your Inner Child

Healing Unresolved Childhood Trauma
& Reclaiming Wholeness through
Self-Compassion

NICOLE JOHNSON, LPC, MEd

New Harbinger Publications, Inc.

Publisher's Note

This publication is designed to provide accurate and authoritative information in regard to the subject matter covered. It is sold with the understanding that the publisher is not engaged in rendering psychological, financial, legal, or other professional services. If expert assistance or counseling is needed, the services of a competent professional should be sought.

NEW HARBINGER PUBLICATIONS is a registered trademark of New Harbinger Publications, Inc.

New Harbinger Publications is an employee-owned company.

Copyright © 2025 by Nicole Johnson
New Harbinger Publications, Inc.
5720 Shattuck Avenue
Oakland, CA 94609
www.newharbinger.com

All Rights Reserved

Cover design by Amy Daniel

Acquired by Jennye Garibaldi

Edited by Kandace Little

Library of Congress Cataloging-in-Publication Data on file

Printed in the United States of America

27	26	25								
10	9	8	7	6	5	4	3	2	1	First Printing

To my son,

Parenting you taught me how to reparent myself. Loving you healed my broken heart. Your light illuminated my path. Your existence inspired me to grow and rediscover joy through your presence. May this book guide others in the healing and nurturing of their inner child in the same ways I have experienced, because of you. I hope these pages bring the same opportunity for healing and freedom as being your mother has brought me.

You are forever what I am most grateful for.

All my love,

Mom

Contents

Foreword — vii

Preface — xi

SECTION 1: Where It All Started

Chapter 1   Introduction: Reparenting Your Inner Child   3

Chapter 2   Trauma: Redefining What Happened   13

Chapter 3   Abuse: The Truth of the Matter   21

Chapter 4   Trauma Responses: Trust Your Symptoms   35

SECTION 2: Wounded Inner Children

Chapter 5   Stages: The Birthplace of Your Wounded Inner Children   53

Chapter 6   Sense of Self: How Your Childhood Experiences Changed You   61

Chapter 7   WICs: Identifying Your Wounded Inner Children   71

Chapter 8   Introductions: Getting to Know Your Wounded Inner Children   79

SECTION 3: Reparenting

Chapter 9	Parenting Styles: How Were You Raised?	91
Chapter 10	Reparenting: In the Here and Now	99
Chapter 11	Reparenting: Your WICs	107
Chapter 12	Reparenting Plan: Staying Consistent to See Success	117

SECTION 4: Growing Up

| Chapter 13 | Temper Tantrums: Setbacks, Symptoms, and Self-Compassion | 127 |
| Chapter 14 | The Impact: Healed Inner Children Help Heal the World | 137 |

| Acknowledgments | 145 |
| References | 147 |

Foreword

Someone once said that it is never too late to have a happy childhood, but it's also never too late to give ourselves the nurturing parenting we have always needed. This is because, in spite of early hardships that created those wounded inner children in us, the larger portion of our personality went on to become a caring, empathic adult. As grown-ups, we naturally give this care to other people and our own children, but we may not realize that we can give it to ourselves as well. We believe that restorative love only works when it comes from others. This may be true in early childhood, but it is not true in adulthood. Love is love, and it heals no matter where it comes from. Surprisingly, some of the most essential healing we need can *only* come from our adult self. In this beautiful book, Nicole Johnson will teach you how to activate and believe in your own healing energies so that you can give yourself what you need to feel whole.

We all have these self-healing energies within us, and you can probably remember times when you've tapped into them and felt relief and new direction. But usually, we find our way to such self-healing by accident: we have a lucky insight, or we get an inspiration. What Nicole will teach you is that we can deliberately access this renewal of life through finding and reparenting those parts of ourselves that have gotten stuck in the traumas and disappointments of the past. Your joy for living may have gotten locked up inside that hurt inner child, and they need you to release it.

If you question the existence of these inner children, I can tell you, after more than thirty years of being a psychotherapist, that they are completely real and their pain runs our lives. That inner child of yours doesn't care if it was decades ago or right now. They just want somebody to see them and respond to them. Your inner child remains expectantly ready to be taken seriously and supported through whatever fears or needs that haven't been addressed. They recognize the grown-up in you as a safe friend and will trust you if you treat them as real and worthy of listening to.

To me, it's a miracle that the human mind knows how to interact with itself to cure its traumas and neglect. To use a medical metaphor in a psychological sense, we are capable of operating on ourselves and making changes that are transformative. We have a growth drive that never stops pushing for wholeness, even if it's been stifled for years. We are ever ready to respond whenever someone offers us a way out of our miseries. But we don't have to wait for a lucky encounter with someone else; we can reconnect ourselves with these positive forces through the process of reparenting our wounded inner child. Nicole will show you exactly how to do that. If you follow her lead and take your inner child utterly seriously, you can claim a do-over any time you want. Now, as an adult, you can say the very words and show the genuine love that you so needed as a child.

Parts work has been recently popularized in therapy by Richard Schwartz, but human beings have always talked to themselves and comforted themselves in the absence of external support. Perhaps we always have sensed our wounded inner child's need for this attention. These internal dialogues and self-reassurances make us feel better, and a little more in control. For instance, in reading this book, I realized that I have been instinctively using Nicole's methods with myself for years. Like many children, I talked myself through difficult times when I felt no one would understand. In adulthood, years after my father was gone, I had a monumental healing conversation with him by imagining him talking with me on the couch. Another time, I listened deeply to my inner child's anxiety and discovered why I needed to change doctors and get better help. These experiences were as real and helpful as any conversations I've had with other people. Life energy for constructive action is released when we treat these parts of ourselves as worthy of being communicated with.

With her gentle, kind way of explaining things, Nicole will *show* you how to trust and communicate with yourself, and how to reassure your inner child that doing the best they could was always enough. Her style of writing reveals a supremely humane soul who will go in there with you and help you dislodge whatever stuck places are causing you pain. She is one of those rare people who is a natural therapist and humanitarian, and I'm so glad that you're about to get the benefit of what I am sure she gives her psychotherapy and coaching clients every day.

There is no filler or fluff in this powerful book; just the information and empathy that you need. She keeps you in charge of your healing process. You get to decide what was traumatic for you because you are the only one who knows how it affected you. She writes to the reader in such an accepting, encouraging way that you feel safe in her hands, carried along effortlessly from one idea to the next. Only later, looking back, will you realize how carefully constructed her narrative is and how her comfortable intimacy makes you trust what she has to say.

You also will feel how much Nicole trusts her readers and their ability to heal themselves. You can tell that she has applied these methods in the real world many times and knows how powerful these approaches are. She spells out how to do these exercises, then steps back to let you experience their healing effect. She offers these approaches to you knowing that you will get the very best from them if only you'll give them a try. From my own experience, I couldn't agree more.

—Lindsay C. Gibson

Preface

The mental health field is inundated with discussions on reparenting and inner child work. However, when asked what it is and how to do it, the answers vary significantly depending on who you are talking to, which is not inherently a problem because healing can come in many forms and many paths lead to wholeness. But as I began my journey of reparenting, as well as my professional deep dive into the concept of inner child work, two recurring issues kept popping up. First, the "inner child" concept seemed nuanced and confusing. Second, the idea of "reparenting yourself" felt weird and uncomfortable. As I spoke with people about their experiences with reparenting their inner child, many said they were struggling to take what they were learning and apply it in their daily lives. And almost everything I read on the topic encouraged, or even required, working with a professional. Reparenting your inner child can lead to such significant healing, growth, and change, so I did not want anyone to miss out on the opportunity because of these roadblocks.

I began collecting data, asking questions, and trying out methods to see what worked and what did not. I wanted to create something comprehensible, practical, and applicable for anybody seeking healing from their childhood wounds and relief from their current symptoms. I wanted to take the convoluted concept of inner child work and help spell it out in a way that was clear and helped people feel comfortable exploring the topic. I also wanted to take the awkward, vulnerable work of reparenting and normalize it, break it into bite-sized chunks, and empower people to trust themselves by trying out what feels right.

Lastly, I will always advocate for people seeking professional support when needed or wanted, but I also understand not everyone has access to or can receive such help. As such, I wanted to provide a user-friendly reparenting roadmap of sorts that allows people to traverse their reparenting journey without having to rely strictly on the help of professionals.

After years of seeing the results of my clients' reparenting journeys, I became desperate to get the word out so that more people could experience the profound transformation I was witnessing. My clients transformed before my eyes in ways that felt like magic. People experienced symptoms decreasing or going away altogether. Confidence bloomed. Boundaries were drawn. Relationships improved. Opportunities unfolded. The once paralyzed and dejected victims of abuse were now marching boldly into their futures, heads held high, victorious. How could I *not* want to share what I was witnessing with the world? I began teaching the concept of reparenting your inner child in group settings, at conferences, on social media, and through my trauma workshop. All around me, people began blooming into the greatest, most healed versions of themselves. As the concept of reparenting your inner child began to spread, more and more people came looking for answers. With that, came the incredible opportunity to write this book.

I do not believe in gatekeeping information and am adamantly against the notion that I, as a mere human who is healing herself, am the answer. I desire to share what I have learned, witnessed, and experienced, but I am merely a person who is *pointing* people toward an answer, toward a solution. A solution that is attainable, realistic, and achievable on your own. This book is meant to be a guidepost on your healing journey. A stepping stone in the story of your life. But you are the hero in this story. You are the one doing the work, facing what you fear, and healing your wounds. I will be with you every step of the way to help cheer you on and remind you that you are not alone, but do not forget that *you* are the answer. *You* are the solution. I hope that with the information in this book, and the free resources provided online at http://www.newharbinger.com/55091, you experience the same healing, growth, and change that I have witnessed in so many others. Because you deserve it. You deserve healing, freedom, relief, and hope. You deserve to receive all the love, support, and protection you may not have gotten as a child. You deserve to have a safe person who loves you unconditionally. And that person is meant to be *you*.

Where It All Started

SECTION 1

CHAPTER 1

Introduction: Reparenting Your Inner Child

The healing journey is much like breathing. Long, slow breaths out. Deep, full breaths in. Exhale. Inhale. Exhale. Inhale. Breathe out pain, hurt, rage, sadness, sorrow, and grief. Breathe in light, love, peace, connection, healing, and happiness. There is a rhythmic, natural, inherent flow to the process. One that we seem to be subconsciously connected to, yet often not aware of. As young children, we intuitively participated in this process. Someone would take our toy and we would freely cry and wail and exhale all of our frustration and fury. Then we would run into the arms of our caregiver and breathe in their comfort, assurance, validation, and love. Well, if we were lucky. Then, somewhere along the way, we stopped participating in that process. Something happened that caused our breath to catch—a sucker punch came in from left field, knocking the wind right out of us—and we stopped breathing.

When we experience childhood trauma—those moments in life that affect us so greatly that they alter us mind, body, and soul—that natural ebb-and-flow process of healing is interrupted. We become stuck in that moment, frozen in time. Holding our breath, unable to breathe. Without an example of what to do or guidance on how to handle what we experienced, we remain stuck, paralyzed, a piece of us lost in that moment, experiencing it over and over again. It can feel like there is no escape and we are doomed to relive our painful past experiences. But as we are all aware, life marches on. So we break away from that memory, often unconsciously, and fracture ourselves emotionally. For survival purposes, we leave a piece of our child-self back in that moment, frozen in time, while we try to move on. Then the next breath-catching moment occurs and we fracture again, leaving another piece of us behind, frozen and breathless. These are our wounded inner children, and this process continues until we wake up one day and feel like we do not even recognize the person in the mirror anymore. We wonder, *What happened to me? Where did I go?* We have unknowingly and all too slowly suffocated ourselves. Cinching off the life force within us that operates from that space of ebb and flow until one day we quite literally, physically cannot catch our breath.

Perhaps you are living life like you are living on autopilot, or maybe you feel like a shadow of who you once were. If this feeling resonates with you, I am glad this book has found you. When we have experienced childhood traumas that we remember and recognize as having been significant, it often can still be difficult to connect the dots as to how those experiences are still affecting us in our here-and-now lives. Other times we disconnect ourselves from those childhood traumas so deeply that we cannot remember them, or maybe we even deny that they happened. This built-in, self-protective response can cause us to not even know what dots we are looking for. Whatever it is that you have experienced and however you may have coped with it, *Reparenting Your Inner Child* is here to guide you to finding and connecting those dots and to show you how to discover your wounded inner child, or children, and reparent them back to wholeness. Together we will sift through the muck and mire of your childhood until we find one of those wounded inner children. We will discover a piece of your child-self stuck in that memory, still frozen in time, and begin the work to heal them and set them free. This book will guide you on how to exhale, release, and let go of the pain your child-self has been holding on to for far too long. You will be shown how to become a safe space for your wounded inner child to run to, rely on, and receive reparenting. And those fractured pieces will eventually integrate back into the whole of you like puzzle pieces finding their fit. With time, the picture of who you were always meant to be takes shape, and the natural ebb and flow of the healing journey will return to your daily life. This journey can be enhanced through active work, so free worksheets that accompany the concepts and exercises within the book can be found online.

So what even is an "inner child"? Where did this notion of reparenting come from? The concept of an inner child goes as far back as the late 1800s with Carl Jung. Known as one of the fathers of psychology and the founder of analytical psychology, Jung discussed the notion of a divine child archetype in his work with Carl Kerényi in the "Introduction to a Science of Mythology: The Myth of the Divine Child and the Mysteries of Eleusis" (1951). He postulated that the milestones of *individualization*, the process of individual development from the unconscious, came from our innate personality, components of our psyche, and, most importantly, the experiences we have in life. From there people began to build on the concept of an inner child and different terminology emerged. In his book *The Wonder Child* (1960), Emmet Fox explores the concept of an inner child that is developed in response to life experiences through a religious lens. The work done by the Janovs in *The Feeling Child* (1975) introduced the notion that we all have an authentic, core self that is responsible for the unfiltered expression of raw emotions. Emotions that are often repressed from childhood and need to be expressed for healing. Then in the 1980s we saw the introduction of the now widely popular Internal Family Systems (IFS) by Richard Schwartz. Schwartz coined the term *exiles* to describe the lost, forgotten, wounded inner children within us that hold the emotions, thoughts, perspectives, pain, and memories of our past traumas (2023). These are just a few examples that capture our collective desire to explore and understand the concept of an inner child for the purposes of healing and growth. Throughout the last several decades, each school of thought has contributed to our understanding of an inner child.

These varying theories had different names to describe the concept of an inner child and different perspectives on its origin, function, and purpose, as well as different opinions on how to interact with or heal this part of ourselves. However, all of these theories seemed to have one thing in common: they all premised that what happens to us in childhood affects who we are today. With that preliminary understanding, methods began to emerge addressing how to heal our inner child and work through childhood experiences. In 1976 Lucia Capacchione developed such a method, which she described in her book called *Recovery of Your Inner Child*. Using a form of art therapy wherein a patient would draw or write with their nondominant hand, Capacchione helped people find, access, interact with, and heal their inner child. She was one of the first to introduce the notion of working to develop a nurturing and positive parent within ourselves while learning how to deal with an inner critical parent so that we could do the "inner family work" needed to care for and meet our inner child's needs (Capacchione 1991). Not long after that, the work of Charles Whitfield in *Healing the Child Within* provided a revolutionary way of looking at how childhood trauma can alter us and what we need to do to heal from it. With more than thirty years in the fields of psychology, addiction, and recovery, Whitfield presented a clear and effective approach to maintaining recovery by healing from childhood trauma and letting go of our "false self" to embrace our "true self" (Whitfield 2006). These are just two examples of how people have sought to help us work through and heal from the complexities of our childhoods.

Inner child work and reparenting therapy are like two sides of the same coin. Interestingly, their paths did not cross as often as one would think, even though they traverse the same woods of woundedness. Reparenting is a concept that stems from transactional analysis (TA). TA surmises that we have three ego states—parent, adult, and child— and emphasizes listening to and interpreting our language to better understand what ego state we are operating from and to work to get into the adult ego state as much as possible (Berne 1989).

In the 1960s, Jacqui Lee Schiff built upon concepts in transactional analysis and introduced the notion of reparenting in a very literal way. Institutionalized patients—particularly those diagnosed with schizophrenia or bipolar disorder and who had significant childhood traumas such as severe abuse, extreme neglect, or total abandonment—spent years working with the same therapists and relived their childhoods by regressing into childlike states and being reparented by their therapists. This total regression type of reparenting included experiences like bottle-feeding, being held, being rocked like a baby, and playing with toys (Schiff and Romulo 1970). Schiff's methods were controversial, helped some, harmed many others, and were largely rejected by practitioners. This led to skepticism, confusion, and resistance to the concept of reparenting for quite some time.

Reparenting is a form of therapy that has largely required the therapist to assume a parental role with the client. As one can imagine, this proved problematic on several levels. Professional lines would get blurred, codependency was easily developed, and transference became unhealthy. In 1974 Muriel James was the first person to introduce the notion of self reparenting and shifted the focus from therapist-dominated to client-directed (James 1985). This method of self-reparenting proved to be safer and more effective than original forms of reparenting. Since then, several different approaches to reparenting have developed but many still emphasize therapist-guided interventions conducted within therapy as well as a focus on reparenting yourself in the here and now. That is where this book differs. Designed so that you are the one in control of your reparenting journey, *Reparenting Your Inner Child* provides you with all the tools, knowledge, and know-how to reparent yourself in the here and now *and* reparent your wounded inner children that are stuck in the traumas of the past.

As inner child work and reparenting methods evolved, so did our understanding of childhood trauma. With each new theory, study, and method introduced, researchers came to understand more and more the tremendous impact our childhood experiences have on development and how current struggles and symptoms can be the cause of long-forgotten traumas from our youth. It is now fairly commonplace to find therapists who walk alongside clients as they unpack their childhoods so that they might be able to reconcile what happened in the past in an attempt to recover in the here and now. There are what I call "the big three" treatments leading the way in this endeavor: Internal Family Systems (IFS), Eye Movement Desensitization and Reprocessing (EMDR), and Trauma-Focused Cognitive Behavioral Therapy (TF-CBT). There is much we can learn from their decades of research, methods, and outcomes. You will find some similarities between "the big three" and the approach laid out in *Reparenting Your Inner Child*; throughout this book, we will pull from their wisdom as we embark on this healing journey together.

Internal Family Systems (IFS)

Although IFS has been around since the 1980s, it seems to have picked up steam in recent years. Found to be particularly helpful in the treatment of PTSD and major depressive disorders, some studies have shown IFS to be more effective than antidepressants (Anderson 2021). Using the concept of a person being composed of parts (an internal family of sorts), IFS guides people in becoming aware of and developing relationships with these different parts. To bring harmony and balance to our family systems and heal our burdened and overactive parts, IFS empowers you to live as your true self (Schwartz 2020). Using IFS, countless people have been able to search within themselves to identify and connect with their wounded, younger parts called Exiles. Similarly, *Reparenting Your Inner Child* helps people to identify and build a relationship with their wounded inner children so that they can successfully reparent them into healing and wholeness. This allows our most authentic selves to re-emerge, and symptoms related to childhood trauma to dissipate.

Eye Movement Desensitization and Reprocessing (EMDR)

EMDR is another highly sought after form of therapy. Considered a best practice with veterans and treating PTSD, EMDR was founded by Francine Shapiro in 1987 almost by accident. As she walked through the park one day, she was plagued with upsetting thoughts and feelings. As her eyes darted around the park she noticed that her unpleasant thoughts and feelings disappeared (Van der Kolk 2015). Long story short and fast forward forty years, EMDR is used across the globe to help people process painful experiences with the use of guided eye movements (similar to that of when we sleep) to decrease, or sometimes even eliminate, symptoms. Like EMDR, strategies outlined in *Reparenting Your Inner Child (RYIC)* help you to work through past childhood traumas and stressful experiences so that you can release the power those experiences have held over you.

Trauma-Focused Cognitive Behavioral Therapy (TF-CBT)

A well-established, evidenced-based form of therapy primarily used with children and parents of children who have experienced trauma, TF-CBT helps guide individuals and families through painful, distressing memories and distorted beliefs. This treatment approach helps people fully process and integrate their trauma so that the related symptoms discontinue (Brown et al. 2020). Seen as a go-to form of therapy by the National Child Traumatic Stress Network, its emphasis on safety, the use of gradual exposure therapy, and the consolidation of the traumatic event helps clients stop difficult symptoms in their tracks. Likewise, the approach in *RYIC* guides you in identifying distorted beliefs, unmet needs, and unhealed wounds from your childhood so that the continuing impact of those experiences loses all power in your life.

These effective therapies are helping people heal in ways we have never seen before. All three come from an understanding that what we experienced when we were young matters. The same is true of this book. *RYIC* presents a unique approach to healing childhood trauma and abuse in a way that combines evidenced-based concepts with an array of different self-healing tools so that you can reparent yourself at your own pace and in your own time. The concepts of this book will guide you to discovering your wounded inner children (WICs) and will equip you with the skills necessary to be the parent you always needed. Stories of clients' journeys will provide you with guidance and validation as you learn to apply the reparenting methods shown throughout the book. Together we will celebrate as you experience the immense healing and growth that comes with reparenting your inner child.

Chapter 1 Takeaways

- Understanding how what we experienced in our childhood impacted us is vital to our healing.

- Inner child work and reparenting therapy have both been around for decades, but never before have the two concepts been merged as they are in this book.

- *RYIC* provides you with the knowledge, tools, and support needed to reparent your inner child or children at your own pace and in your own time.

Questions to Consider

- Have you attempted any childhood healing methods? If so, what has helped and what has not?

- What questions do you have about RYIC? Write them down so you can answer them as you read and learn.

- When you think about the concept of reparenting your inner child, what emotions do you feel?

CHAPTER 2

Trauma: Redefining What Happened

When you hear the word "trauma," what comes to mind? If you are like most people I have worked with, worst-case scenarios probably flood your thoughts. War. Assaults. Catastrophes. The tendency we have to reserve the word for experiences we consider terrible enough to be called trauma is one of the biggest hindrances we have in our healing journeys. This is particularly true of childhood traumas. Take a moment to think about what comes to mind when you read the words "childhood trauma": do you believe trauma involves only the experiences that are the stuff of nightmares? If so, you are not alone; that perspective is not uncommon. However, the limiting definitions and narrow perspectives held toward "what counts" as trauma cause many of us to dismiss the adverse childhood experiences that are still affecting us in painful or challenging ways today.

If you are someone who has courageously acknowledged, worked through, and healed from your traumas, often a milestone in your healing journey is feeling safe enough to speak out about your experiences. But all too often, victims seeking to help others by speaking up about their experiences are met with gatekeepers of the word trauma. Individuals who tell trauma survivors that what they experienced was *not*, in fact, traumatic and that they were *not* traumatized. If you have experienced this, I see you, and I am so sorry that happened. You did not deserve such a response. Your experiences and how they affected you are real and valid. Unfortunately, these gatekeepers feel entitled to make such a bold accusation because the trauma survivor's experience does not fit the rigid definition of trauma they cling to. The funny thing, though, is that leading schools of thought, mental health organizations, and professionals in the field cannot even seem to *agree* on the definition of trauma.

In my psychoeducation course on trauma and abuse, "Get a G.R.I.P.," I share with the group members the varying definitions of trauma and how these definitions can hinder our ability to identify the traumas in our lives. Let us look at some of those definitions. Pay particular attention to not just what is being said, but what *is not* being said.

- "Any disturbing experience that results in significant fear, helplessness, dissociation, confusion, or other disruptive feelings intense enough to have a long-lasting negative effect on a person's attitudes, behavior, and other aspects of functioning. Traumatic events include those caused by human behavior (e.g., rape, war, industrial accidents) as well as by nature (e.g., earthquakes)..." (APA Dictionary of Psychology, s.v. "trauma").

- "An event, series of events, or set of circumstances that is experienced by an individual as physically or emotionally harmful or life threatening and that has lasting adverse effects on the individual's functioning and mental, physical, social, emotional, or spiritual well-being" (Substance Use and Mental Health Services Administration, s.v. "trauma").

While our definitions regarding trauma have certainly improved over the years, they still place a large emphasis on our life being threatened, physical injury, or a specific, horrific event. While all of those things can and do cause trauma, they are not *all* that causes trauma. These limitations are problematic for the millions of people who are suffering from trauma-related symptoms due to experiences unrecognized. How can we heal something that we cannot even properly label?

To add insult to injury, many people will seek professional help for their suffering only to experience feeling further disqualified and confused. This is because the criteria that professionals use to diagnose mental health disorders is the Diagnostic Statistical Manual (DSM-5-TR). While the DSM-5-TR does not define what trauma is, it does set forth the criteria that must be met for someone to be diagnosed with a trauma-related disorder—and the criteria can be incredibly specific. For example, to qualify for a diagnosis of Post-Traumatic Stress Disorder (PTSD), the first box to check states you must have been exposed to "death, threatened death, actual or threatened serious injury, or actual or threatened sexual violence" (First 2022). This extremely narrow gateway of PTSD-inducing experiences causes countless people to be disqualified right out of the gate. This disqualification can be invalidating and re-traumatizing for people seeking help. Victims of traumatic experiences, particularly in childhood, tend to already face dismissal or denial from others, and minimization by their own brains. This diagnosing domino effect is a serious problem that reparenting your inner child endeavors to solve by providing you with a more inclusive definition of trauma and the power to decide for yourself what experiences, situations, or circumstances were traumatic in your life. You alone should be the one to decide that, and ultimately you alone hold the power to make that declaration. It can be incredibly validating and deeply relieving to ignore the naysayers and validate your own pain by declaring, "That *was* traumatic for me!"

If you are someone who has struggled to understand why your symptoms persist and why your suffering continues, I encourage you to explore your thoughts on trauma with me. If I were to ask you, "Do you have a history of trauma?" what would you say? If your answer is "no," why is that? Is it because you did not experience something severe like physical or sexual abuse? Those are not the only traumas that exist. If I told you that your pervasive and pesky symptoms like constantly worrying, being easily startled, chronic anxiety, and hyperindependence might be PTSD related, how would you respond? Would you balk and scoff, dismissing the notion because you were never in a war or natural disaster? Post-traumatic stress-related symptoms are not reserved for only our war heroes and catastrophe survivors. Too many people are suffering in silence and confusion because they are living with trauma-related symptoms and do not realize it. Have you ever found yourself saying, "Sure I had issues in my childhood and problems with my parents, but I had a roof over my head, clothes on my back, and food on the table"? While these things are vital to our survival, they do not exempt you nor protect you from experiencing childhood traumas.

Anna's Story

Anna is a forty-year-old female who has been happily married for almost two decades and has two twin children who are her world. She is successful in her career, having worked her way up the corporate ladder in a male-dominated field, where she has settled into a high-level director role. She has healthy relationships with family members, a decent social life, is well-liked, beautiful inside and out, educated, articulate, and funny. She came to me several years ago, already on medication for stop-her-in-her-tracks anxiety, and wanted to work on "handling life better." She had tried a handful of therapists, all of whom focused primarily on her anxiety by using Cognitive Behavioral Therapy methods and worksheets. She had experienced mild success with this approach, but it never seemed to last. Her intake paperwork denied all forms of trauma and abuse (according to the criteria listed). Despite Anna facing terrible anxiety at work and physical health issues from her nonstop, go-go-go lifestyle, interestingly, Anna only ever talked about her father in session.

Her dad was a successful, hard-working, well-respected salesman for an international company and had been a closet drinker for a while. His drinking had spiraled out of control, as these things often do, and

Trauma: Redefining What Happened

a few months before Anna's thirty-seventh birthday, her dad was pulled over driving home from a Christmas party and slapped with a DUI. Anna's world tilted on its axis. Anna had always looked up to her father, admired him, respected him, and "defended him," as she put it. "Defended him from whom?" I asked one day. Anna looked puzzled and sat contemplating my question for a moment. "My mom, I guess," she replied. "You had to defend your dad's drinking to your mom?" I clarified. "No," Anna stated flatly, "I've had to defend my dad my whole life, for everything and anything...to my mom." Anna went on to describe how growing up, her controlling, critical, and often cold mother had always harped on her dad and made Anna feel unwanted and a bit unloved, even though those words were never directly spoken to Anna by her mother.

Anna and her father, on the other hand, were thick as thieves her whole life. He adored her and she cherished their time together. Which, as it turns out, was limited. Her father traveled for work weekly, leaving little Anna home alone with her mother when she was a child. Then one day, when Anna was about ten, her father informed her that he was leaving her mother—and subsequently Anna. He said he simply could not deal with Anna's mother's "ways" anymore. Then poof, he was gone, and Anna was alone. Anna tells the story straight-faced and emotionless. When I asked how her father leaving her affected her as a young child, she replied that she simply "understood why he left." She discussed how she would have left too but she couldn't because she was a child.

A few sessions later Anna was in a panic. She was going to be interacting with some bigwigs from high up in her company—all male, all older—and she was *terrified*. There was one superior in particular that she wanted to be sure to win over. "What if he doesn't like me? What if I make a fool of myself? What if I am not good enough?" My response to Anna's distress caught her off guard. "Don't think, just respond—what is the worst that could happen?" "He could leave me," she blurted out. Anna and I stared at each other silently for a moment. I repeated the words back to her slowly and deliberately. "He...could...leave...

17

you." It was a lightbulb moment. Anna's eyes welled with tears, the first real emotion she had ever shown in a session.

From that moment on, Anna was no longer resistant to examining her childhood. She began to unpack the dynamics of her upbringing and how those dynamics influenced her life and the woman she developed into. She allowed herself to explore how those experiences helped mold her, for better or for worse, into the person she is today. Anna made connections between her fears at work, her issues making female friends, and her intense need to take care of her father with how she had been wounded as a child. Anna went from denying a history of trauma to recognizing that she had experienced several traumas in her childhood. That recognition allowed Anna to finally be able to deal with what had been plaguing her and address the cause of symptoms she had long since suffered from. Anna is a prime example of how a narrowly presented view of trauma can lead to confusion, self-blame, misdiagnoses, and, worst of all, unnecessary prolonged suffering. Anna's journey of reparenting her inner child was a turning point in her life and a path of healing she continues to walk today. But the anxiety that crippled her? Gone.

So where does that leave us with this complicated concept of trauma? In the next several chapters I am going to discuss what trauma and abuse can look like, particularly in ways we haven't been taught to recognize. We are also going to explore trauma responses, correlating symptoms, and how they impact us. These are vital first steps to take in identifying our wounded inner children so that we can reparent and heal them. However, none of that matters if we do not first get on the same page regarding what trauma actually *is*. Without a clear definition, we might miss identifying something as having been traumatic. If we are unable to identify that something was traumatic, we will not recognize what our trauma response was. Without understanding what our trauma response was, we will not be able to understand the correlating symptoms we may very well *still* be suffering from. See how that cycle can keep us stuck? This cycle causes endless suffering, a lack of change, and hopelessness. It causes us to remain lost in our wounds, merely surviving through life instead of thriving. And frankly, we simply deserve better. So with that being said, let us take our first step in this healing journey and define trauma in a way that allows us to acknowledge and validate our experiences so we can begin to heal from them. RYIC's definition of trauma is an event, circumstance, or situation (acute or chronic) that is distressing to an individual and causes an impacting emotional response, often long-lasting.

Chapter 2 Takeaways

- The disqualifying definitions of trauma have caused many of us to overlook experiences that wounded us, leaving us stuck in confusion and pain.

- Trauma is still stigmatized, and that can cause us to deny or dismiss experiences we have had that were traumatic because they were not "bad enough."

- RYIC encourages you to give yourself permission to decide what was traumatic to you based on how you feel it impacted you and not some textbook definition or stereotype.

Questions to Consider

- When you hear the word "trauma," what comes to mind?

- Do you feel you have fallen prey to stereotyped or stigmatized types of trauma? In what ways?

- What experiences from your childhood are you realizing were traumatic to you based on RYIC's definition of trauma that you did not previously recognize? Write these down for later!

CHAPTER 3

Abuse: The Truth of the Matter

When you hear the word "abuse," what comes to mind? What does the term evoke in you? Take a moment to reflect on your immediate thoughts and emotions related to this concept. As we learned in the last chapter, the way we define and perceive concepts like trauma influences our ability to recognize it. The same is true of abuse. Whenever someone courageously decides to embark on their journey of reparenting their inner child (or children), I encourage them to take the time to reflect on their beliefs regarding trauma and abuse as a first step. This is what I am encouraging you to do now. This first step is important because, all too often, unhealed wounds go unnoticed or dismissed due to a narrow understanding of what constitutes abuse. Similar to our exploration of trauma in the previous chapter, it is essential to examine the current definitions of abuse we have to work with and how they influence our ability to identify abuse in our own lives. Let's take a look at two common, yet very different, definitions of abuse:

- The Oxford Dictionary states abuse is "to use something improperly…" (Oxford English Dictionary, s.v. "abuse").

- The American Psychological Association (APA) characterizes abuse as "interactions in which one person behaves in a cruel, violent, demeaning, or invasive manner toward another person or an animal" (APA Dictionary of Psychology, s.v. "abuse").

Let's flesh these out a bit, shall we? As we unpack these definitions of abuse, I encourage you to consider how you may have applied these definitions to your experience and whether that has been validating or disqualifying.

Let's look at abuse as "the improper use of something" first. For this definition, swap *something* for *someone*—you. When you hear this definition, what comes to mind? As a child, did anyone ever improperly use you? An obvious example of this would be sexual abuse. A not-so-obvious example would be an emotionally immature parent who conditions their child to feel responsible for the parent's emotional stability. This is the improper use of a child emotionally. This is abuse. If you are unsure what an emotionally immature parent is, what that looks like, or if you had one, I encourage you to read Lindsay Gibson's best-selling book *Adult Children of Emotionally Immature Parents*. What other ways might you have been improperly used in your life?

Now let's look at the APA's definition of abuse. While it is a more inclusive definition, we can hyper-focus on words like "violence." While abuse obviously includes violence, of any kind, it also includes the act of being *cruel*, *demeaning*, or *invasive*. Cruelty tends to be reserved for describing heinous acts, but cruelty can be very sneaky and therefore very sinister. To be cruel is to cause pain or suffering, often willfully and with no concern. Cruelty is not only when a parent says mean and degrading things to their child ("You were an accident, I never wanted you!") but *also* when a parent says nothing. Cruel is the parent who withholds words that would impart value and a sense of belonging to their child. Cruelty is rejecting a request for connection and sending a crying child to their room, isolated and dysregulated. To be cruel is to be abusive.

Fleshing out these definitions and applying them to our lives is not exactly a joyride, so if you are feeling uncomfortable or doubting yourself, that is okay! Take your time, take a break, and when you are ready to come back, remember that *not* doing this work can render us unable to see clearly where our hurt is coming from. Expanding our perspectives of abuse allows us to properly label experiences from our childhoods that wounded us. This is an important step because wounds left unlabeled are left unhealed. When we can label our painful childhood experiences for what they were, abusive and traumatizing, we can now begin the process of healing them. This relabeling causes our healing journeys to move along with greater ease, less confusion, and longer-lasting results. To help you with this process, I have broken abuse down into seven categories that you can use as a guide as you identify and label unmarked childhood experiences.

The Seven Types of Abuse

As we go through these, keep in mind that some abuses can fall into multiple categories and this is not a complete list. As you read through, take note of any memories that come up, especially ones you never considered before!

Neglect

Neglect is an abuse that is woven into all forms of abuse. Neglect is not what was *done* to us, it is what was *not done* to us. It is the absence of what is needed, whether that be due to the refusal or inability to meet our basic and vital needs. Think of basic needs as things like food, water, shelter, air, and physical safety, and vital needs as things like love, affection, support, guidance, belonging, and mental or emotional safety—just to name a few. When these needs are not met we are experiencing neglect. Neglect can be:

- **Physical:** Lack of affection, nurturance, comfort, or safe touch
- **Financial:** Withholding of financial support as punishment or lack of financial means to meet needs
- **Social:** Lack of social opportunities, social abandonment, or being socially ostracized or rejected
- **Emotional:** Withholding of love, affection, and emotional support
- **Psychological:** Lack of validation or guidance, or withheld affection

PHYSICAL ABUSE

Physical abuse can be obvious acts such as assault. This includes hitting, kicking, rough handling, or physical punishment (yes, this includes spanking), but it also includes:

- Involuntary isolation: Sending an upset child to their room
- Restricting movement: Putting a child in timeout for prolonged periods
- Not tending to medical conditions: Refusing to take a child to the doctor
- Misuse of medication: Overmedicating a child to make them more manageable
- Forcible feeding or withholding food: Requiring a child to eat something they don't want to or sending them to bed hungry

Far too many people claimed they were never physically abused because their caregivers "never hit them." However, when we reflect on all that physical abuse includes, many of us are unable to hold to that claim any longer. It can be jarring to realize that you were physically abused and neither you nor your parents even realized it, so remember to take it slow and give yourself time to process.

SEXUAL ABUSE

Sexual abuse is not limited strictly to sexual acts between an adult and a child. It can include any experiences wherein you were treated cruelly or were abused or hurt regarding your sexuality, your sex-related body parts, or your beliefs regarding sex. Sexual abuse can include:

- Molestation, rape, sexual assault, and forced or pressured non-consensual sex
- A lack of proper sex education that results in increased risk
- Not believing a child or blaming them when they disclose sexual abuse
- Child-to-child sexual acts

As you reflect on experiences that impacted you negatively (even if they do not fit "the mold" of classic sexual abuse), I encourage you to validate them because they matter. This can be a very triggering area to explore, so take your time and go at the pace you feel comfortable with.

FINANCIAL ABUSE

This form of abuse is more common in adult relationships, but we sometimes see it in parent-child relationships as well. Situations where a parent might use money to try to "buy" their child, or withhold resources to meet basic needs as a form of punishment, are forms of financial abuse. Examples include:

- A parent who refuses to financially pay for an extracurricular activity (such as dance, choir, or theatre) because they insist their child play a sport instead
- Not buying a child much needed clothes because they didn't take care of a pair of shoes
- Making a child pay for things that are inappropriate to their age or needs

This type of abuse can often subject a child to further abuses like ridicule, shame, humiliation, and bullying by others outside the home, such as peers, extended family, even strangers. The motive, intent, and impact are important factors to consider when reflecting on financial abuse in your childhood.

SOCIAL ABUSE

We often see social abuse such as bullying present in peer-to-peer relationships with children, but social abuse can also be:

- Parents who refuse or limit social interaction with friends (social interaction is vital to a child's development)
- Publicly shaming or humiliating a child
- Sabotaging the child's social connections

Remember, if it was cruel, hurt you, or impacted you negatively, then you have permission to let it count as abuse. Nothing is too small.

The last two, emotional and psychological abuse, are where I want us to take a deeper look. It is not uncommon for people to seek therapy for what we call "Big T" traumas. These are big, obvious traumas such as physical or sexual abuse. Rarely do I see people seek therapy for the "little T" traumas. Unfortunately, "little T" trauma is where emotional or psychological abuse hides (although I would *never* call them little).

Sadly, people with wounds in these areas often do not even know it. They might seek help for anxiety, depression, or relationship issues not knowing the cause. They often feel hopeless and treatment is ineffective. If this resonates with you, you are not alone. You are not broken, healing is possible, and there is an answer. Sometimes the answer is found in the hidden wounds held within the hearts of our emotionally and psychologically abused wounded inner children. So let us take a look and see what we can find.

EMOTIONAL ABUSE

Emotional abuse can include both what is *done* and what is *not done* to a child. Remember what is *not done* is also neglect. Emotional abuse includes overcontrolling a child, isolating them, and being dismissive toward their emotional needs. It also includes:

- Name-calling/Insults: "You are such a spoiled brat!"

- Blaming: "I wouldn't yell if you would listen the first time!"

- Intimidation: "Stop crying or I will give you something to cry about!"

- Shaming: "I can't even look at you right now!"

- Humiliating: "Stop acting so weak, toughen up!"

- Criticizing: "How many times do I have to ask you!"

- Emotional Neglect: "Go to your room and do not come out until you are calm!"

Maybe you did not have a parent who called you names or criticized you, but were they ever dismissive toward you, your interests, or connection requests? Maybe your caregivers did not shame you, but did they allow you to have healthy emotional expressions like crying, being angry, or displaying big energy when happy? Often, parents do not realize that they are being emotionally abusive, and social expectations of what we find acceptable can also play a role in parenting. Studies have shown that parents begin treating their male children differently than their female children starting around age four. This can include disallowing emotional expressions not viewed as acceptable based on gender such as sadness or anger (Sharman et al. 2019). Not being allowed to cry because you are male, or be angry because you are female, is emotional abuse. Emotions are not gender specific and you have a human right to feel *all* of them.

PSYCHOLOGICAL ABUSE

Psychological abuse is the most covert of all; it is often not recognized because it flies under the radar. Psychological abuse can take a toll on us that rivals the worst of the more obvious abuses. Due to its hard-to-spot methods and invisible impact (it leaves no physical mark), it is often the most long-term abuse endured by its victims. Often called childhood psychological maltreatment (CPM), it includes emotional neglect, frequent criticism, isolation, intimidation, terrorization, belittlement, and withheld affection (Sharman et al. 2019). It can also include:

- Parentification: Treating a child like an adult or giving them the responsibilities of one

- Stonewalling: Giving a child the silent treatment or refusing to communicate

- Gaslighting: Manipulating a child into doubting their perception, reality, or experiences

- Exposing a child to domestic violence: Being verbally or physically abusive in front of a child

- Turning a child against someone: Trying to make the child hate the other parent

In a study done out of the University of North Texas, Watts and his team discovered that CPM is a significant risk factor in developing *lifelong* PTSD, and people who experienced CPM suffered from more severe PTSD-related symptoms than people who experienced physical or sexual assault (Watts et al. 2023). This information is often shocking for people as we still place a huge emphasis on the "big T" traumas and overt abuses and tend to dismiss the covert abuses or "little T" traumas. This is not to say, of course, that these traumas and abuses do not have a profound impact. They absolutely do. But what *is* being said is that you could be suffering from severe, chronic, debilitating post-traumatic symptoms and never have had a hand laid on you.

We must recognize that to be criticized or have affection withheld, to be dismissed and told you are to "be seen and not heard," to be sent to your room or told to stop crying, to be treated with disrespect or less than human because you are a child is abuse—often traumatic abuse—and it can give you a whole host of painful, life-long symptoms. So what happened to you, "big" or "small," matters, and you need to *let* it matter. Give your childhood experiences the weight they deserve and the attention they need. Without doing so, *many* wounded inner children will remain lost, frozen inside of you, crying for help. Do not let them be met with the same indifference and dismissal that created them in the first place.

DeMINDs

Embarking on your reparenting journey involves identifying childhood experiences you may have overlooked. Our new perspectives on trauma and abuse have given you the roadmap to get started. However, a word of warning as you venture down this path: you might bump into roadblocks. These roadblocks are what I call DeMINDs. DeMIND stands for Deny. Minimize. Normalize. Defend. These roadblocks are a result of what I call "abuse brain" and reflect a process we go through when we are trying to understand something we have experienced from a different perspective. A mental battle ensues as we work to come to grips with the truth of our experiences. Experiences that we once thought were "not that bad," but we are now coming to realize the opposite. Let's walk through DeMINDs together so that you can feel equipped to overcome them and come out the other side victorious!

Denial

Reflecting on your childhood, you may feel inclined to deny any abuse. You might think, *I know people who were actually abused and I didn't go through what they went through, so I wasn't abused.* This is denial. I encourage you to remember that just because someone has a life-threatening illness and you have the flu does not mean you are not sick simply because you are not *as* sick as them. You still need treatment and healing. I encourage you to give yourself permission to acknowledge the abuse you experienced. Admitting it does not make you feel worse; it simply connects you to the pain that is already inside of you so that healing can begin.

Minimization

Minimization is a tool our brain uses to cope with overwhelming experiences. When minimizing, you might say, "It wasn't that bad," "They never hit me," or "It was only once." Out of fear for how we might feel if we accepted the reality of our experience, we minimize. Children often have no choice but to do this. But it is important to remember that you are not a child anymore and your wounded inner children need you to validate what they went through in order to heal. Give yourself permission to acknowledge the reality of your childhood and your perspective of your experiences without feeling dramatic or wrong.

Normalization

As children, our home lives, experiences, and environments were all we knew. With nothing to compare our lives to, our brains concluded that *this* is the way the world is. Our childhood environments became our programming for what is "normal" or familiar, and our brain loves familiar. In fact, it is wired to seek what is familiar. This is often why, as adults, we repeat relationship dynamics that we had with our parents as children—with partners, friends, and employers. To challenge our beliefs of what is normal, to disrupt our initial programming, can be perceived as threatening to the brain and deeply uncomfortable to the body. Give yourself permission to recognize that what was considered normal may not have been acceptable and allow yourself to admit that you deserved better.

Defending

Children have a biological wiring that compels them to seek love, acceptance, and belonging with their caregivers. This wiring can cause children to defend even abusive caregivers. This instinct is often carried with us into adulthood. I have seen people defend their parents' abusive actions even in the worst case scenarios. For many of us, we did not experience worst-case scenarios so we are even *more* inclined to be defensive. Maybe you had a parent who tried their best but had their own unhealed trauma. Maybe you know they never would have *intentionally* hurt you. Maybe you are close with them now and you are afraid the relationship will be negatively impacted. For these reasons and many more, we can find ourselves stuck between defending our parents' abusive behaviors while simultaneously trying to heal from the impact those behaviors had on us. Give yourself permission to release the need to defend. Healing does not require that you villainize people, ignore their intent, or end relationships. What it does ask is that you believe and support your wounded inner children so that they can heal, and you can finally be free.

Hannah's Story

At age twenty-four, Hannah came to me feeling as if she had lived a lifetime and had nothing left. She was riddled with crippling anxiety, felt unmotivated and depressed, and had no idea who she truly was. On the inside, she felt lost, confused, and hopeless. On the outside, Hannah was a brilliant young lady and was in school to become a pediatric dietician. She came from a financially stable family, had great friends, and appeared to "have it all." Years of coping skills, affirmations, and empowerment podcasts had gotten Hannah nowhere and she was desperate for change. However, Hannah's perspective on trauma and abuse had her denying any trauma, minimizing any abuse, normalizing her experiences, and defending her parents. She was stuck.

One day Hannah casually mentioned her dad repeatedly abandoning her and her mom's expectations of perfection. When I pressed, she brushed it off, saying she was "over it." But minutes later, Hannah's face was beet red and she was nearly hyperventilating. I encouraged Hannah to examine the potential connection between her mysterious physical symptoms and the moment she was talking about her childhood. It would be several sessions of similar occurrences before Hannah would work through DeMINDs well enough to see the truth. Hannah realized that she had been experiencing psychological and emotional abuse since she was two years old. Abandonment, emotional neglect, criticism, parentification, belittlement, dismissal, invalidation, and isolation were so commonplace they felt completely normal to her. Hannah's childhood was riddled with traumatic abuse, but it had gone unnoticed and unaddressed because no one had ever raised their voice or even laid a hand on Hannah. And yet Hannah's trauma-related symptoms had been off the charts for years. Through patience and self-compassion, she began validating her experiences and connecting with her wounded inner children. As she courageously loved herself enough to do the healing work, Hannah began to come to life.

Her symptoms decreased, the light came back into her eyes, confidence exuded from her voice, and her true self came forward. Her journey of reparenting her inner children was hard-fought and well-won.

This is the journey you are now on.

Chapter 3 Takeaways

- Abuse encompasses physical, sexual, financial, social, emotional, and psychological acts as well as neglect. It can also be overt (very obvious) or covert (not obvious at all).

- Childhood psychological maltreatment (CPM) can lead to severe, chronic PTSD, sometimes surpassing the impact of physical or sexual assault.

- The concepts outlined in DeMINDs may surface during the exploration of childhood experiences, requiring patience and self-compassion.

Questions to Consider

- Were there instances of abuse in your childhood that you may not have been aware of or previously considered abuse? If so, what were they? Write them down!

- Do you find yourself experiencing DeMINDs when reflecting on childhood memories? Why might this be?

- What would it mean for you to validate your painful childhood experiences? Does such validation bring relief and understanding or perhaps stir up doubt or fear about what comes next? Embrace your feelings; they are valid!

CHAPTER 4

Trauma Responses: Trust Your Symptoms

> "Trauma is not what happens to you but what happens inside you."
>
> —Gabor Maté, *The Myth of Normal*

When we think of trauma, often we think of the event and overlook our *response* to that event. People diminish another person's suffering by saying, "Well *my* trauma was worse than *your* trauma," because their event was worse. People argue that the word trauma is misused when labeling an event as traumatic that was not "bad enough." This argument dismisses people's unique experiences based on faulty criteria. Comparing traumatic events and only acknowledging the ones that appear more severe in obvious ways is invalidating and can be retraumatizing for those who are equally suffering from experiences less recognized. Trauma is a whole-being experience. It is not *solely* the event, but also the way in which that event or experience impacts us. The event can be what strikes the match, but trauma is the fire that burns *inside* of us. A fire that can burn long after the event has passed. To be able to put out that fire, we need to understand why it started, what fuels it, and why it keeps coming back even after all our efforts. Let's dive in.

Shifting Gears

Our bodies have this brilliant, built-in alarm system called the autonomic nervous system. Its response is lightning fast and it can hijack your body without your permission. Since birth, it has been working in tandem with your brain to identify threats and learn how to respond accordingly. This system is responsible for your survival, your continued safety, *and* much of your suffering. Imagine that your body is a car and your nervous system is the gears. Your brain can shift your nervous system into different gears as needed for your survival. When all is well, we are in neutral, coasting along. This gear reflects our parasympathetic system, or a "rest and digest" state. We are calm, relaxed, and healing. But when our brain perceives danger, it shifts our nervous system out of neutral and into action. This takes us out of a parasympathetic state and into a sympathetic state, or an "arousal state." Here is what the gears look like:

- First Gear: *Alert*. There is a potential threat and you have become focused and aware.

- Second Gear: *Alarm*. There is a threat and your system is telling you to respond.

- Third Gear: *Panic*. There is imminent danger and you need to take action immediately.

- Fourth Gear: *Distress*. You are in active danger or life-threatening harm and the focus is survival.

These gears are biological responses to danger, perceived or real. They are what fuels the fire within us. Think about times in your life when you have experienced one or more of these gears. What did each of these gears feel like inside of you?

Trauma Responses

When we are experiencing something traumatic, our gears shift and we respond to that traumatic experience. We have a trauma response. If you have heard terms like fight or flight, then you have heard of trauma responses. However, there are several different trauma responses that we experience apart from the commonly known fight or flight. We are going to examine six different types of trauma responses. When experiencing any of these, we can be in any of the different gears. As you read through each of them, see if you can think of an example. It can be a personal example or one you may have witnessed, read about, or seen in a movie.

Flock

This often unknown trauma response is specific to situations that involve a group of people. It is sometimes referred to as "herd mentality" because everyone moves together. We see this with animals as well. That is because there is safety in numbers but also because people often are unsure what to do or how to respond so they "go with the flow." The goal of the flock trauma response is to find safety and to have power in numbers. During this trauma response we often experience sensations such as panic, confusion, fear, aggression, terror, and overwhelm. An example of this trauma response is the 2017 Las Vegas shooting during the Route 91 Harvest music festival when a man opened fire on concertgoers from the thirty-second floor of a nearby hotel. In the chaos, confusion, and panic, people instinctively followed each other, looking to group movement to see what direction might lead to safety.

Freeze

This trauma response is exactly what it sounds like. During this trauma response the brain hijacks your executive functioning and paralyzes you. The goal of this trauma response is often to collect data and assess the situation in order to know which next action is best. But it can also be a default response to terror and confusion that can sometimes be dangerous. Some schools of thought say that the trauma response of freeze is a part of our "shutting down" process. We will look at that process during the last trauma response. However, the sensations that accompany this trauma response show that the exact opposite is happening. During the freeze response our eyes are wide to take in information, our hearing is more acute, our heart is pounding, our blood is pumping, our muscles are tense, and it can sometimes feel like time slows down. An example of this trauma response is a deer in the woods who hears a noise and freezes in place. We also see this depicted in movies when people see something they never have before and stand, frozen in place, as the threat moves toward them.

Flight

When we think of the trauma response of flight, most of us think of someone fleeing, running away, or escaping a situation. But this is only one aspect of flight. We can also have the trauma response of flight mentally and emotionally. The goal of this trauma response is to get you out of the situation and to safety as quickly as possible. This trauma response is one of action so it comes with really intense physical sensations. Feelings of anxiety, panic, terror, and desperation accompany physical symptoms of shaking, trembling, rapid breathing, and your heart pounding or beating rapidly. This is largely due to the levels of adrenaline coursing through your body. This hormone is released into your body by your adrenal glands, at the command of your brain, with the intention of getting you to *move*. However, we need to recognize that not all situations that trigger the trauma response of flight require us, or even allow us, to physically flee. You can have a flight response to getting an email from your boss asking you to come to their office. Or as a child when your parent called your name sternly and you had to go to them. We can also want to flee our thoughts or emotions that are too painful or do not feel safe to feel. When we have the trauma response of flight but there is nowhere safe to run away to, the toll it can take on us mentally, emotionally, and physically can be severe.

Fight

The trauma response of fight is on the flip side of the same coin as the flight trauma response. It is also an action-oriented trauma response and therefore uses adrenaline in the same way. However, with the fight response the goal is to defend or protect yourself or others from threat of harm. We often think of physical threats and therefore physical defense, like being attacked, jumped, or assaulted. But the threat of harm can also be mental or emotional. If we are being gaslit, manipulated, invalidated, emotionally abused, or verbally threatened, we can have the trauma response of fight just as we would if someone were physically attacking us. This often appears like an overreaction, which abusers can then use to victimize themselves. (This is called reactive abuse.) With the trauma response of fight we experience "hot energy," anger, rage, rapid breathing, impulsive action, or feeling out of control. Examples of people somehow fighting off a bear or flying into a blind rage when someone harms their child are examples of the fight trauma response.

Fawn

The fawn trauma response is where we see things change significantly and pendulum swing in the opposite direction of the previous trauma responses of flock, freeze, flight, and fight. Those trauma responses come with big energy and often result in external action taken. With the fawn trauma response the opposite happens. Fawning means to seek approval or acceptance by use of means such as flattery. But when it comes to the trauma response of fawning, what we are really doing is negotiating for our safety by any means necessary. Fawning is one of the most common types of trauma responses among children because children cannot flee or fight. They have no choice but to develop alternative ways of trying to stop, prevent, or mitigate whatever abuses or traumas they are experiencing. The trauma response of fawning results in action taken in an attempt to stabilize a situation, appease an abuser, or stop harm from being done. The most common result of fawning that we see is people pleasing. Many people believe that they are a born people pleaser, that it is just a part of their personality. Society often applauds those who people please, saying they are selfless and self-sacrificing for the sake of others. When all the while many people pleasers are simply stuck in the cycle of fawning—always feeling unsafe, unable to escape, unable to fight, pleading for their safety. Sensations that accompany the trauma response of fawn are suppressed emotions, intense anxiety, desperation, fear, loneliness, and making one's self small. The term "walking on eggshells" is often used to describe people who are in a fawning trauma response. Defending our abuser, minimizing the abuse, or convincing ourselves we deserve it also come with the fawning trauma response. An example of the fawning trauma response is a child who is constantly seeking the approval of their emotionally neglectful or immature parent. The child changes who they are, their likes and dislikes, becomes performative in school or sports, stays out of the way at home, and learns to take care of themself as to not to be a burden. All of these efforts are an attempt to negotiate with the parent to not hurt them, be that mentally, emotionally, or physically.

Flop

The trauma response of flop is often the least acknowledged or talked about trauma response. It is sometimes lumped in with freeze; however, they have diametrically opposite symptoms. The lack of education regarding this trauma response has caused countless people to blame themselves for what they experienced and labor hate toward themselves for how they acted. That is because the flop trauma response looks completely different than all the rest. With this trauma response we do exactly what the name sounds like. We flop, we collapse, we sometimes faint, we "give up." We don't fight, we don't try to escape, we don't scream for help. We *endure* it. This trauma response is our way of withdrawing from reality when we are facing imminent, inescapable pain. While often physical in nature, it can also be an attempt to escape mental or emotional pain. The goal of this trauma response is to simply survive. We see this trauma response very clearly in the animal kingdom. An opossum will play dead. A goat will faint. When we experience the trauma response of flop our body shuts down instead of revs up. Our heart rate slows, our blood pressure drops, our blood pools to our vital organs leaving our hands and feet freezing cold. During this trauma response our body might go limp, we might feel as if we are withdrawing from reality and going inside our body, and sometimes we feel as if we are leaving our body, often floating above it. The most common symptom associated with the flop trauma response is dissociation, which, simply put, is the act of us disconnecting. An example of the trauma response of flop is when someone goes limp and does not attempt to fight or stop a sexual assault. Too many people have hated themselves, thinking they allowed this, or experienced victim blaming, being told "they must have wanted it because they didn't fight." When they were actually experiencing a very real and very valid trauma response that they had absolutely no control over. If you relate to this in any way I want you to take a minute to pause and say to yourself, "It was not my fault. There was nothing I could have done. I was doing what I needed to do to survive." And remember, if you are here reading this book, then you *did* survive. Your trauma response worked and you made it through.

Summary of Trauma Responses

Now that you are familiar with the different types of trauma responses and what they can look like, here is a summary for your reference. You can use this summary to refresh your memory as you work on the Trauma Responses worksheet in the free resources.

- **Flock**—herd mentality, everyone moves together
    - Sensations: alert, panic, confusion, fear, aggression
    - Purpose: to find safety and have power in numbers
- **Freeze**—frozen in place like a deer in the woods who hears a twig snap
    - Sensations: focused, enhanced vision and hearing, blood pumping, time slows down, poised to take action
    - Purpose: to paralyze you so your brain can collect data and assess the situation in order to know which action to take
- **Flight**—escaping, fleeing; can be physical, mental, or emotional; a rabbit running from danger
    - Sensations: adrenaline, shaking, heart pounding, rapid breathing, anxiety
    - Purpose: to get you out of the situation and to safety as quickly as possible

- **Fight**—aggressive action taken to defend or protect oneself; a cat attack
  - Sensations: hot energy, anger, impulsive action, feeling out of control
  - Purpose: to defend oneself from threat of harm (can be mental, emotional, or physical)
- **Fawn**—other-focused action to stabilize a situation; a nervous dog rolling on its back in submission
  - Sensations: making yourself small, careful movements, suppressed anxiety, desperation, fear, people pleasing
  - Purpose: to negotiate for your mental, emotional, or physical safety
- **Flop**—withdrawing from reality when facing imminent inescapable pain (mental, emotional, or physical); opossum playing dead
  - Sensations: slowed heart rate, dropped blood pressure, cold extremities, fainting, loose body, going inside or floating above oneself
  - Purpose: to survive

Checking In

Take a deep breath and ask yourself, *How am I feeling?* Do a quick body scan and notice any sensations you are experiencing. Often when talking about or learning about trauma responses it can sometimes illicit the accompanying sensations. If you are experiencing that now, take a break, take some deep breaths, remind yourself that you are safe, and come back when you are ready. This is a lot of information to take in and often we can have memories come back, experience flashbacks, or feel like we are reliving the experiences that caused the trauma responses. The book will be here when you are ready; giving yourself some time and space to digest what you just learned is most important. This is a beautiful way to take a step toward loving yourself just a little bit more.

Sometimes people only validate trauma responses for extreme situations such as fighting in war or fainting in a catastrophe. Or they think that people have trauma responses *only* to physical danger. That is not true. Many people have never experienced extreme situations or been in physical danger but have had a lifetime of experiencing trauma responses. That is because it is not the severity or type of event that determines whether or not we have a trauma response. Any time we experience a threat (real *or* perceived) and danger (of any kind) we will instinctively respond. Many people do not realize that the brain can and does respond to a mental or emotional threat (like criticism or neglect) the same way it would a physical threat. Danger can come in mental, emotional, social, financial, and spiritual forms, not just physical. When you experience a threat to your safety, of any kind, you shift gears and react to that threat. That reaction often comes in the form of a trauma response. A response to the trauma you are experiencing. No one has the right to tell you that you did not, or are not, experiencing a trauma response. You are the one living inside of your body so you are the only authority who can declare what it is you experienced.

Understanding what trauma responses are and how we can have them in response to *any* type of threat can help validate our reactions. If you overreacted or responded in a manner outside of your character, hopefully you can recognize that your response was not because you were weak or a bad person: you responded in such a way because you were in an altered state of functioning. You were having a trauma response. This insight brings you clarity, self-compassion, and the release of shame and guilt. This information can also help you identify your default trauma response. Did one of the trauma responses stick out to you more than the others? Do you always want to avoid or escape situations that make you anxious (flight)? Or do you have a habit of caring more about keeping others happy than speaking up for yourself (fawn)? If those responses worked in the past, they can become your default reaction to potential threat or harm, even if it does not make sense to the logical part of your brain. When we respond in ways we do not understand, often our default is to judge or criticize ourselves: *Why didn't I just speak up?* or *Why did I run away? I should have taken a stand and defended myself!* These self-deprecating thoughts pile onto the pain and do not help us to heal. But when you understand that your brain picks the trauma response, not you, and that maybe your brain picked that response because it has worked in the past, then hopefully you can release some of that self-condemnation and allow compassion to flood in.

Trauma Response Symptoms

We have looked at what happens when we are experiencing a traumatic event that illicits a trauma response in the moment. But what about when the traumatic experience has passed but you still feel like you are living in that first gear of being on constant alert or feel stuck in fight or flight mode? A lot of our suffering comes from perpetual and chronic trauma responses that continue to happen long after the event is over. The fire inside is still burning. In order to be able to put that fire out, we need to understand why this happens. To protect you from future potential harm or re-experiencing what you went through, your brain will mark or flag various aspects of the distressing experiences of your past for future reference. It can flag just about anything, such as images, sounds, smells, places, people, emotions, sensations, locations, dates, and so forth. When you encounter or experience one of these flagged aspects from previous experiences, you can get *triggered*. And when you become triggered, your nervous system shifts gears because it senses a threat. This often results in a trauma response. If we are not aware of what triggers us (encountering those flagged aspects from previous traumas), we can feel out of control, confused, overwhelmed, or even "crazy." Here is an example: loud footsteps down the hallway meant danger to you when you were a child. Even though you are now grown up, when you hear loud footsteps (the flagged aspect) you get triggered (and your nervous system shifts gears), and in response you freeze with fear (trauma response). See how that works?

Trauma responses come with symptoms. A list of symptoms is provided on the Trauma Responses worksheet in the free resources, but here are a few to give you an idea:

Irritability, hypervigilance, exaggerated startle response

Conflict avoidance, social anxiety, people pleasing

Trouble sleeping, nightmares, intrusive thoughts

Headaches, stomachaches, chronic ailments

If you experience any of these symptoms and you have struggled to understand why, ask yourself these questions: What gear am I in when I experience these symptoms? What is the trigger that causes me to shift gears? What past experience is that trigger tied to?

This is important work because when we do not understand what is happening within us or why, we can feel "broken" or helpless. We slip into shame, confusion, or even despair. But with understanding comes precious relief. Something is fueling that fire and once we know what it is, we can begin the process of putting it out. This gives us hope for change.

Trauma Responses and Our Wounded Inner Children

If you had a stressful childhood, an emotionally immature parent, or your needs were unmet, then you probably shifted gears frequently and trauma responses might have been so common they felt normal. The normalization of trauma responses can cause us to become numb or desensitized to them. Sometimes we even begin to believe that trauma responses are who we *are*. All too often people mistake their trauma responses for personality traits. We think we are docile with a desire to please others, not realizing we are fawning. We pride ourselves on our hyper-independent, introverted lifestyle, not realizing we are in perpetual flight mode. These qualities can, of course, be personality traits, but when you have had childhood trauma it can be hard to tell the difference between how you have learned to behave to survive versus how you tend to act due to who you are. If being wounded was all you knew, it can be difficult to identify your wounded inner children when they look just like you. However, understanding trauma responses can help us realize that who we are is *not* our symptoms and those symptoms are often cries for help from our wounded inner children.

Eric Gentry, an expert in traumatic stress, teaches that we perceive a threat when there is none based on painful past learning (Gentry 2022). Our painful past learning (traumatic childhood experiences) causes us to perceive a threat when there is none (those pesky flagged aspects) and shift gears in response (trauma responses). This is why you can be safe but still experience a trauma response. This is why, even though your traumatic experience was thirty years ago, you are still suffering from symptoms caused by that event. Think of it as your wounded inner children crying out for help because something about *this* situation points to pain from *that* past situation even when they're not quite the same.

Brené's Story

This story is not from a client but rather from an esteemed author, researcher, and wonderful human—Brené Brown. In her book *The Gifts of Imperfection*, Brené recounts when she was invited to speak to parents at a public elementary school about their involvement since she was an expert on relationships, connection, and authenticity. She recalls how she immediately knew something was off. After inquiring with the principal and receiving no explanation, she blamed her nerves. During the principal's introduction, she was trying to "stave off vomiting and talking [her]self out of running." The principal's tone toward the parents was off-putting and almost aggressive, and Brené mentions that "in hindsight" she should have said something but did not. The parents were unreceptive to her message and one parent in particular was next-level disruptive. Brené explains how she desperately tried to impress the parent, becoming animated and loud, all to no avail. When her presentation concluded, she tucked tail and ran to her car to get out of there as quickly as possible. She described having a hot face, a racing heart, intrusive thoughts, dry mouth, and tunnel vision, and that time felt like it was slowing down (Brown 2010).

Can you see them? Did you spot the trauma responses? Brené Brown, the fierce queen of authenticity, was shifting gears and experiencing trauma responses like fawning and flight. We can't know for sure what Brené's painful past experiences might have been that influenced her responses to the situation, but we *can* relate, can't we? Imagine yourself in her shoes. What would glares, loud voices, defensive vibes, and unimpressed people cause you to feel? Unwelcome? Inadequate? Rejected? Would you feel humiliated, defensive, unworthy, or ashamed? Think about times in your life when you have experienced those feelings. Are those painful memories? This is how a seemingly harmless situation can cause us to have a trauma response and experience the correlating symptoms.

When was the last time you had a trauma response? What were the triggers, how did you respond, and what symptoms did you have? What memories are those triggers tied to? When we use our current symptoms as clues to lead us back to the birthplace of our pain, it is there that we find our wounded inner children waiting for us, wanting and ready to heal.

Chapter 4 Takeaways

- We have a brilliant built-in alarm system that will instantaneously shift gears inside of us without our permission to keep us safe. It is not the enemy and we do not want to shut it off. Our goal is to understand and work with it.

- There are six types of trauma responses (flock, freeze, flight, fight, fawn, flop). We can have a default trauma response or have experienced trauma responses for so long that we think the symptoms are normal.

- Encountering aspects of past traumatic experiences can trigger us into having a trauma response even if we are safe.

- Even Brené Brown has trauma responses, so there is hope for us all.

Questions to Consider

- What trauma response(s) resonate with you?

- How do you know which gear you are in? Which gear do you feel you spend the most time in? Write out descriptive words for each gear, including neutral.

- What trauma response symptoms did you think were your personality but you now realize are not? What can you say to yourself now that you realize the truth?

Wounded Inner Children

SECTION 2

CHAPTER 5

Stages: The Birthplace of Your Wounded Inner Children

People invest countless hours and considerable money working through *what* happened to them, which is crucial to healing. But all too often, the *when* aspect of what happened gets overlooked, which causes us to miss vital information for healing. This is particularly true when dealing with childhood traumas. So let us explore *when* something happened to us and how the "when" influenced our experience's impact on us. This step provides the information needed to identify specific wounded inner children and begin getting to know them.

Our childhoods are often a blur: vague recollections and painfully clear memories jumbled together like a tangled ball of yarn, which makes identifying and working through painful past experiences difficult. However, compartmentalizing our childhoods into blocks of time provides a structure that gives context to muddy memories and untangles confusing knots. These blocks of time that we are going to use are called "Erikson's Stages of Development." Erik Erikson was an American psychoanalyst who dedicated his life to researching childhood development. His work became a guideline for understanding how biological, psychological, and social factors impact our development throughout life (Erikson 1994). Erikson created eight stages that examine our development from birth until death, though we will be looking at the first five that focus on childhood.

Stages of Development

Development is our mental, emotional, and physical progression as we grow and age. Erikson's stages, categorized by age brackets, identify the development that is occurring within that stage. For example, mental development can involve forming beliefs, emotional development can involve expressing feelings in age-appropriate ways, and physical development can involve learning how to walk. The stages also highlight what influences our development for better or worse. Influences that are positive and appropriate help us successfully pass that stage. In doing so, we develop a virtue (or strength). Influences that are negative or lacking interfere with our development at that stage. As a result, we develop a maladaptive trait (a way of coping with what we lack). Each stage is marked by a significant event we are experiencing and a general question that we are asking. When all goes well, we progress through the stages, developing strong virtues, healthy beliefs, and a clear sense of self. However, when life circumstances, environmental factors, and deficits in our caregivers negatively impact the stages, our development is interrupted, we develop maladaptive traits and negative beliefs, and our sense of who we are becomes injured. Let's look at a breakdown of each stage.

Stage one takes place from birth to eighteen months old and is called "Trust vs. Mistrust." The development that is occurring during this time is a sense of trust in others and that our needs will be met. We are asking, "Can I trust others to meet my needs?" This question is answered by our caregivers tending to and meeting our needs. The event that captures this is feeding. If our needs are met with consistency and regularity, we will develop a sense of hope within us (the intended virtue). We develop trust and a sense of safety and security. If our needs are not met or are inconsistently met we become mistrusting and withdraw. This is the maladaptive trait we develop to deal with the fear of not getting our needs met and the sense that the world is unsafe and people cannot be trusted.

Stage two is from eighteen months old to three years old and is called "Autonomy vs Shame." The development that is occurring is a sense of independence and autonomy. We are asking, "Can I do things myself?" We explore this with potty training, dressing ourselves, and playing with toys. If we are allowed the space, safety, and sense of control to answer this question affirmatively, we will develop the virtue of will (think a "strong-willed" child). If we are not permitted freedom or are consistently scolded or criticized for our actions, we will develop the maladaptive trait of compulsion. We will act out, go against instruction, and feel the need to rebel. We also begin to experience shame, a painful sense that something is inherently wrong with us.

Stage three is "Initiative vs Guilt" and takes place from three to five years old. Here we move beyond exercising control over our bodies to exerting control over our environments. We do this primarily through interactive play such as picking the game, telling others what to do, and fighting over toys. We are asking, "Am I good or bad?" When our caregivers provide clear boundaries for safety, teach us appropriate behaviors, and encourage us to feel empowered, we develop the virtue of purpose. We feel capable and have a sense of purpose within our family. If we are in a controlling, strict environment or are frequently punished for our attempts to expand, we develop the maladaptive trait of inhibition. We feel a sense of guilt that how we act is wrong and we inhibit our desire to express ourselves.

Stage four is called "Industry vs Inferiority" and spans from roughly five to thirteen years old. During this stage, we develop a sense of pride in our abilities and accomplishments. This is done primarily through social interactions with peers at school or through extracurricular activities. We are asking, "How can I be good?" Success in this stage develops competence, a belief in our skills, and abilities to handle tasks. However, if we are unable to develop these skills or experience a major life disruption, we may instead develop passivity as a maladaptive trait. We doubt our ability to be successful and stop trying.

The final stage in childhood, stage five, takes place from thirteen to around twenty years old and is called "Identity vs Confusion." It is during this time that we finalize our sense of self (more on that next chapter) and develop a sense of personal identity. This is done through social relationships, particularly with peers. We are asking, "Who am I?" If given the space and freedom to answer this question successfully, we will develop the virtue of fidelity—staying true and faithful to who we are. However, if we are forced to conform, are shamed or judged for who we are, or are rejected, we will develop the maladaptive trait of repudiation. We will reject ourselves, deny who are, and become insecure.

Checking In

How are you feeling after reading through the stages? Pay attention to memories that come up or experiences you recall. Reviewing our childhood through the lens of these stages can bring up questions about why we are the way we are—a worksheet called Stages of Development is provided to help you map out your answers. Maybe you have always carried shame, believing you are unlovable. But what did stages two and three look like? Were you encouraged to express your emotions and praised for your efforts? So maybe it's not that you are inherently unlovable; maybe your development was wounded and you are still suffering. Understanding how our stages were affected allows us to see ourselves in a more compassionate light. What we thought were personality traits we now realize are maladaptive traits. What if the aspects you judge yourself for the most are simply wounds that need to be healed? And what if there is a way to revisit those stages to complete development so that your maladaptive traits fade away and your virtues begin to bloom?

Stages and Wounded Inner Children

The stages help map out *when* something happened so that you can better understand how that experience impacted you. Pinpointing these experiences by stages also clues you into your wounded inner children, or WICs, who are still stuck in that stage, paralyzed and needing reparenting. Instead of simply having wounds from childhood, you now can see specific WICs. Four-year-old you, who loves bananas and hates bath time, is trying her best to behave out of fear of being hit. Nine-year-old you, with teeth falling out and an obsession with Barbie, is sobbing because the kids at school were ruthless. Sixteen-year-old you is pretending to like sports and partying so she does not have to face the sting of rejection and ridicule. No longer is it just a painful memory, but rather a wounded child you have discovered within yourself. A WIC who is very much alive, hurting, and needing your help to heal.

Keep in mind that several factors affect your stages of development. Cultural influences, societal norms, gender roles, birth order, social status, and access to resources all play significant roles in childhood development. Maybe you experienced displacement or relocation, suffered the loss of a loved one, or had a tragic accident that was no one's fault. Or maybe you had the best-intentioned caregivers who loved you deeply but, due to their own unhealed trauma or life circumstances, failed to meet your needs, and the gap between your needs and what they could provide you affected your development. If you struggle to validate your WICs for this reason, remember this statement: Impact over intent. Meaning that when it comes to healing, the impact an action has is more important than the intent behind that action. Our WICs are not born solely of *intentional* abuse or neglect.

57

WICs created by *unintentional* painful experiences are just as real and deserve to be acknowledged.

On the other hand, we can sometimes pendulum swing from invalidating our wounds to feeling like we're villainizing or blaming those who wounded us. Understanding that *this* action by *this* person hurt you in *this* way, does not mean you are villainizing them. Explaining how another's actions impacted your development is not the same as blaming. Sometimes our WICs *are* mad at how they were treated and need us to validate their perspective and pain. Feeling like we are blaming others can stop us from validating our own experiences, which can impede our healing. Our ability to successfully develop throughout childhood is almost entirely dependent on the behaviors and choices of our caregivers, particularly in the first three stages. Let us hold space for that truth without feeling like we are blaming others to villainize them so that we can hear what our wounded inner children have to say.

Lastly, if you feel like acknowledging your WICs means you are obligated to confront the person who wounded them, remember that this work is between you and you. Sometimes people decide to address those who wounded them, but sometimes that is not possible or safe. It is also not necessary to heal. You can do this work privately and at your own pace. What *is* important is allowing your WICs to tell you what wounded them and understanding how the "when" impacted you. So, when you are ready, review the stages of development and assess how you fared. What stages were negatively impacted? In what stages do your WICs live? What strengths do you want to develop and what maladaptive traits are you ready to heal from?

Lark's Story

Lark had been through decades of off-and-on counseling. She was incredibly intelligent and self-aware but had never found relief from her severe emotional suffering that caused physical problems. Despite the chronic abuse and neglect endured throughout her childhood, Lark's memory was remarkably intact. This made the process of identifying her wounded inner children simpler but overwhelming. Lark did not know where to start. The stages of development provided structure so she could see her WICs clearly. Instead of replaying the painful memories ad nauseam, Lark used the stages to explore how her childhood experiences impacted her. She made connections between the maladaptive traits she possessed and what childhood experiences birthed those traits. She was able to finally reconcile that just because her parents "did their best" didn't mean their choices did not wound her. She began healing from the impact of her experiences because she finally acknowledged the wounds they caused.

For the first time, Lark felt hope. She could not do anything about what had hurt her, but she *could* do something about how it continued to hurt her. Lark worked through each stage, validating and reparenting her WICs into wholeness through self-compassion, patience, and safety. And wouldn't you know it? The virtues from each stage began to bloom from within her. Her answers to the stages' questions changed in ways that brought relief, peace, and self-love. She also experienced a reduction in both emotional and physical symptoms, so much so that her health improved significantly.

Chapter 5 Takeaways

- The "when" of a childhood traumatic experience matters as it impacts our development.

- There are five stages of development from birth to adulthood. Success within a stage develops a virtue. Impacted stages can impair development and result in maladaptive traits. We can heal these traits and develop the virtues.

- We can use the stages to identify our wounded inner children and validate their experiences, perspectives, and pain without blaming or villainizing anyone.

Questions to Consider

- Which stages were impacted positively and which ones were impacted negatively? How so?

- Which virtues and/or maladaptive traits do you see within yourself?

- Do you have any painful experiences you invalidated because there was no malicious intent?

CHAPTER 6

Sense of Self: How Your Childhood Experiences Changed You

When you hear the expression "sense of self," what do you immediately think of? Is it personality traits or characteristics? Maybe you think of someone confident and self-assured. If you are thinking something along these lines, you are on the right track. The concept of a sense of self is a little nuanced and we often do not take the time to learn what it is and how it is developed. However, understanding what sense of self is and evaluating yours is an integral part of your healing journey. Sense of self work will empower you to more effectively reparent your wounded inner children in a way that allows the true you to come into full bloom.

The American Psychological Association defines a sense of self as "an individual's feeling of identity, uniqueness, and self-direction" (APA Dictionary of Psychology, s.v. "sense of self"). It is sometimes referred to as our self-concept, which is our ability to describe and evaluate our characteristics, traits, skills, roles, and the like (APA

Dictionary of Psychology, s.v. "self-concept"). In essence, it is our sense of identity. It is important to understand that our sense of self is not *just* the characteristics that comprise us, it is the *awareness* of those characteristics. This difference may seem small, but it is crucial to grasp, for without it, we miss the whole point.

Contemplate this question: how aware are you of what makes you, *you*? No, I am not talking about your job title, your role as "mom," or who you are to other people. Can you assuredly describe the factors that make up who you are? The values, beliefs, perspectives, attitudes, quirks, and characteristics that are uniquely you. Not ones you adopted from others, or wear as a mask to fit in, and not the residual symptoms of wounds. How confident are you that you truly know who you are, have been, and will be? How well can you answer these questions free from doubt or second-guessing yourself? If you are crystal clear and unwavering in your awareness of who you are, you can probably skip this chapter. But if not, I encourage you to keep reading.

In the previous chapter we explored Erikson's stages of development and the idea that *when* something happened impacted our development, which influenced who we were and maybe still are today. Similarly, the experiences we had growing up influenced our sense of self. In fact, our childhood experiences play such an influential role in our sense of self that Erikson believed that much of our self-identity was established by stage five, the final stage of development within childhood (Erikson 1994). So let us traverse once more into our past, this time through the lens of our sense of self. But before we do I want to give you a bit of good news. At no point are we stuck with or trapped by our shortcomings. If you start feeling discouraged because you see areas that were wounded or weakened, or you find yourself thinking, *I don't have any idea who I am!*, I want you to take a deep breath, give yourself some love, and remember—we are moldable, adaptable beings who are capable of miraculous transformation, deep healing, and self-development. The story of who you are is not over!

The Six Factors

Six factors comprise your sense of self. Think of them as the framework for the house that is you. The inside of your house is all the decor that makes up you: your beliefs, values, opinions, perspectives, passions, hobbies, interests, and so on. The interior of your house is influenced by the strength of that framework—the six factors. Here is a breakdown of each one, how they are defined, and examples of when a factor is strong or impaired:

- Agency: a sense of being in control of yourself
    - *When strong:* you know that your thoughts, emotions and behaviors are yours
    - *When impaired:* you feel like your beliefs, feelings, or choices aren't really "you"
- Continuity: the sameness of essential features over time
    - *When strong:* you stay consistently who you are over time
    - *When impaired:* you feel as if you change who you are depending on who you are with
- Coherence: being a complete and unified person
    - *When strong:* you have a confident sense of who you are as a unique individual
    - *When impaired:* you feel like a shell of a person, that you blend or aren't real
- Completeness: feeling complete in and of yourself
    - *When strong:* you feel whole independently of external relationships
    - *When impaired:* you feel empty, like there is no real you, especially without the presence of external relationships

- Authenticity: knowing your true self and owning it
  - *When strong:* you feel comfortable expressing who you really are
  - *When impaired:* you feel as if you are masking, faking it, or playing a part in life
- Vitality: a state of well-being, aliveness, and vigor
  - *When strong:* you predominately feel alive, present, and have a zest for life
  - *When impaired:* you feel chronically depressed or dead inside

I encourage you to pause and rate each factor on a scale of 1 to 10, with 1 being you feel like you do not possess that factor at *all* and 10 being that you fully possess it. Take a look at that list. What factors are high? What factors are low? What factors feel confusing or muddled? Now ask yourself *why*. Why is one factor low and another high? Why are you clear on some and confused on others? When you are ready for the next step, allow yourself to contemplate what childhood experiences you had that influenced your scores. Pay particular attention to any factors that are below a 6. It can be especially helpful to review the stages of development and contemplate what experiences you had, how you were treated within that stage, and how it may have influenced your sense of self. For example, if you were raised by a narcissistic parent who insisted that you live to make them proud, make them look good, and your identity was nothing more than being an extension of them, your sense of authenticity may have never even had a chance to develop. Or maybe you felt you had to consistently change yourself—your interests, hobbies, passions, and the like—in order to be accepted by loved ones. How might this have impacted your sense of continuity?

If you are doubting whether or not your answers are "correct," remember that there are no wrong answers, and that doubt you are feeling might speak to your sense of coherence being impaired. So now you have a place to start! Understanding where your sense of self is strong or impaired, and where you are confused are all valuable insights into yourself. This kind of compassionate, self-reflective legwork makes knowing where to focus, where we want to start, or what is most important in our healing journeys easier to identify.

Now, if you find yourself thinking something along the lines of, *Wow, I really suck*, I want you to read these next few sentences very carefully.

First of all, no, you do not suck. Say, OUT LOUD, "I do not suck." Now say it again.

Second, remember that we are practicing self-compassion first and foremost. So say OUT LOUD, "I am worthy of compassion and give it to myself now." One more time, say it again.

Lastly, it is important to recognize that the development of our sense of self is a naturally occurring phenomenon and, if uninterrupted by trauma or neglect, tends to develop well. If you feel your sense of self is impaired it does not mean anything is wrong *with* you; it means something happened *to* you. So, say OUT LOUD, "Nothing is wrong *with* me, something happened *to* me." You know the drill—one more time.

An article from 2020 reviewed the literature on the concept of sense of self and what the research says about it. Not surprisingly, trauma, abuse, and developmental neglect have a tremendous impact in decimating those six factors and, therefore, the person we become (Basten and Touyz 2020). The research also shows that an impaired sense of self is a risk factor for diagnoses such as borderline personality disorder, narcissistic personality disorder, dissociative disorders, eating disorders, and chronic depression. In working with clients suffering from an impaired sense of self, it was exceedingly common that they were also suffering from:

- Being fearful and distrusting of others
- A chronic desire to withdraw or isolate
- Feelings of shame, guilt, self-doubt, and self-blame

- A deeply held belief that others are better than them or they are less worthy than others
- Struggling with being passive, avoidant, and fearful of confrontation or conflict
- Fear of new experiences, quitting of hobbies or habits often
- Doubting their abilities, and ignoring their accomplishments because nothing was ever good enough
- Being a "chameleon" by taking on the personality of others around them to be accepted
- Having insecure attachments, unhealthy relationships
- Chronic codependency in relationships and being easily manipulated by others
- Personal growth that felt stunted or blocked
- Feeling confused about their purpose or feeling a lack of purpose
- Feeling lost in life, hopeless, or despondent
- Believing that something is inherently wrong with them or that they are "broken"

If you are thinking, *So then* everyone *has an impacted sense of self?* You are not alone, and you are not wrong. Some people experience an easier unfolding and some people take hit after hit. But no one gets out of this life unscathed. The experiences we have impact us, the situations we go through shape us, and our upbringings program us for better or for worse. While those hardships are difficult, our life experiences are not the problem when it comes to our sense of self. The problem is we continue to suffer from the symptoms of an impaired sense of self because we mistake those symptoms as personality traits, as inherent aspects of who we are. We think, *This is just who I am*, and consequently writhe in self-loathing, judgment, despair, and pain.

Instead, we are going to change our thinking to reflect the truth. We are going to say, "My sense of self was impaired by my experiences and because of that I have been suffering from these symptoms. But that ends now!" This reframe brings relief, ushers in self-compassion, and gives up hope. There is such healing when we leave the land of "this is just the way I am" and step into the land of "that is who I was, I wonder who I will now become!" There is such freedom when we finally understand that "I'm not a timid pushover who can't stand up for myself...my sense of agency was impaired because I was bullied!" Seeing the gap between where we want our sense of self to be and where it currently is gives us a blueprint for reparenting ourselves. Since much of your sense of self was influenced by how your caregivers treated you, imagine the ways you will heal, grow, and thrive when you finish raising yourself in the manner you needed, so that your sense of self can improve. Having answers to why we struggle gives us hope that things can change, and that hope is felt by every single one of your wounded inner children.

Can you feel their excitement?

Lily's Story

Lily was one of the most self-aware clients I had ever encountered. She was in graduate school to become a counselor at the time so there was not anything that I could tell her that she did not already know. She had an answer as to why she did anything and everything. The problem was that nothing was changing, and she was suffering from debilitating anxiety, bouts of crushing depression, and a sense of general unrest in her life. Lily and I worked together for many months before she was willing to talk about her childhood. She had already shared with me her Big T traumas, the ones that (in her mind) were to blame for all her symptoms. When I inquired about her general day-to-day life as a child and her relationship with her parents, "It was fine" was always the default answer.

One day Lily casually mentioned how she felt unsure of herself as a mother because her daughter was becoming a teenager and she was not sure how to parent her. This led to a conversation about her own teenage years. Lily said it was uneventful because she was basically alone. By the time she was thirteen her mother was "traveling for work" (which she later learned meant having an affair) and her father was gone for weeks at a time. So she was on her own the majority of the time. She was responsible for getting herself to and from school, extracurriculars, and events, as well as maintaining the day-to-day tasks of upkeeping a house and taking care of herself. She lived in terror of people finding out, so she worked to hide the fact that she was vulnerable and lied to people about her situation. She also had an eating disorder, was suffering from severe PTSD from a sexual assault, and was using substances to cope.

My stunned-to-silence reaction gave her cause to pause and reflect and thus began the journey of peeling back the layers of Lily's sense of self. What Lily thought were self-aware answers were just deflections. She realized that all the self-hate and shame she carried about who she *thought* she was were symptoms of an impaired sense of self. A sense of self that took a hit in every factor, in every way, for many years. As Lily made the connection between her experiences then and who she was at that point in time, the shame, guilt, self-hate, self-criticism, and feelings of hopelessness slid right off of her. She wasn't depressed for no reason; she lacked vitality because she had been stuck in survival mode for decades. She was not hyper-independent and inflexible; she had a super strong sense of agency from having to go it alone most of her childhood. She overcompensated with certain factors to make up for the ones that were wounded. Lily worked to reparent her wounded inner children by focusing on strengthening sense-of-self factors she never had the chance to develop. This brought about harmony and balance to her sense of self, and with it clarity and love for the person she was now, and excitement and hope for the person she was becoming.

Chapter 6 Takeaways

- Your sense of self is composed of six factors that are like the framework of a house, and inside are all the little details that make you, you. Your *awareness* of these factors and details is key.

- Your sense of self is impacted by the experiences you have, particularly in childhood. As adults, many of us think, *This is just the way I am*, but as we heal from our childhood wounds our sense of self strengthens.

- Knowing that you are not your symptoms and that you have the power to become your true self gives you hope, relief, a sense of safety and freedom, and reinvigorates your zest for life!

Questions to Consider

- Write out every characteristic you can think of that makes up who you are. Which of them might be symptoms of an impaired sense of self and not an inherent personality trait? Circle them.

- Which of the six factors do you feel drawn to work on first? Why do you think that is?

- Close your eyes and imagine a version of you that has a strong, healed sense of self. What is that version of you like? What's different? What's changed? How does it feel when you observe that version of you?

CHAPTER 7

WICs: Identifying Your Wounded Inner Children

We have spent the last six chapters learning the truth about what wounds us (trauma and abuse), understanding that *when* we get wounded matters (stages of development), and how being wounded impacts us (trauma responses and sense of self). You have courageously traversed one of the hardest parts of the reparenting journey and did not even know it. The next step is to connect all those dots to get a clear picture of our wounded inner children, which is what this chapter is for.

Just like in any relationship, you would not offer advice or try to help without knowing the person first, what they needed, and how they would respond. The same is true when working with our wounded inner children. So before we can begin reparenting them, we need to get to know them. It is important to take time to gather details about your WICs so you can understand how best to reparent them and help them heal. To get started, we need to take a "roll call," meaning we need to try to identify all the WICs within us that are ready for healing. There are two ways to do this. The first is starting at the beginning and working forward. The second is starting with where you are now and working backward. You can do one, the other, or both, in any way that feels right for you. Remember, there is no right or wrong way to do this internal work, and trusting yourself to follow the path that feels right for you is a huge part of this healing journey!

Childhood Timeline

The first option is to create a timeline. You can create your own or use the Childhood Timeline in the free resources provided online. Either way, you want to have a line that represents your childhood, birth to adulthood. Make a tick on the timeline to represent any adverse experience that you recall (or were told) that you feel wounded you. If you had a season of your life when you experienced ongoing stress or lasting pain, you can use a single tick mark to represent that time in your life. It can be helpful to use the stages of development as mile-markers for different experiences or to identify the age you were. You can also find a breakdown of the stages of development in the free resource online. Next to the tick mark, make a little note about yourself. For example, one tick mark might say "age 4, loss of a caregiver," and another might say "teenage years, never felt heard." It can be as general or as specific as you like. Here is an example:

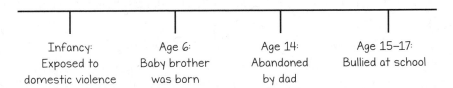

Backtracking Symptoms

The second option for identifying your wounded inner children involves backtracking your symptoms. Meaning you start with current symptoms you have and work your way backward into your childhood.

This is helpful for people who struggle to recall their childhoods, have vague memories, or want to improve their connection with the sensations in their bodies. Start by making a list of all the symptoms you feel you currently struggle with. These symptoms can be anything that you suspect might not be the *real* you, but rather a lingering sign of an unhealed wound. They can also be sensations, mindsets, or internal struggles you deal with. If you have already worked to reduce or alleviate some symptoms, but are still wanting to understand their origin, you can list them as well. Once you have listed the symptoms, follow the five steps below for each symptom in order to identify a wounded inner child. If you have a lot of symptoms or the symptoms feel overwhelming, take it slow and at whatever pace you are most comfortable with.

1. Take a deep breath, close your eyes, and focus on the symptom and how it presents in your body. What does it feel like? Where do you feel it?

2. Write down descriptive words for what you noticed in your body and where (sharp, heavy, chest, shoulders, and so on).

3. Say out loud to yourself, "When are other times in my life I have felt these sensations?" Trust what comes up, allow memories to float back into your awareness, and be patient and compassionate with yourself. You can revisit this step as many times as you need.

4. Write down the memories or insights that come up. It is okay if they are fragments or a vague knowing.

5. Place those experiences on the Childhood Timeline so you can get an idea of the different ages you were when you experienced these symptoms. It is okay if it is general or a guesstimate.

A worksheet called Backtracking Symptoms is provided online. Here is an example:

1. Symptoms I experience: anxiety, fear, and sometimes anger all mixed together

2. Sensations: I feel a tightness in my chest, trouble breathing, my hands shake, but I refuse to cry

3. Memories: I have had these sensations most of life but I remember it happening a lot during my teenage years and at night as a little kid, maybe around five

4. WICs Identified: an angry sixteen-year-old me, and a scared five-year-old me

It is important to note that not every symptom we experience is because of or directly tied to a WIC. You may already be aware of some symptoms that are due to other reasons. We are not invalidating that. This exercise is for you to identify *if* your symptoms are tied to a WIC, particularly those pesky symptoms that you have been plagued with for so long and seem to have no source. But this data-collecting step is not just about identifying specific WICs; it is also an exercise in self-compassion, self-trust, and self-love. Which is crucial to the reparenting journey. Every time you write down a memory you are unsure of, you validate your pain. Every moment you spend connecting with your inner experience, you are strengthening your relationship with yourself. When you pause and put the book down because you sense you need a breather, you honor yourself.

When we identify pain we felt as a child, we can sometimes re-experience those emotions or sensations in the present moment. That can sometimes feel scary or overwhelming, but it is okay! Nothing has gone wrong, you are not making it worse, and it is not for nothing. Remember, that pain and those emotions have been inside of you all along. You are simply allowing yourself to connect to those emotions and pain *so that* you can process through them in order to release them and ultimately heal. This is often not our favorite part of the healing journey but it is work that cannot be passed over. We cannot go around our pain or skip to the end result. The only way out...is through.

So take a deep breath, and keep going.

Rachael's Story

Rachael came to me because of Pedro Pascal. Like millions of other people, she had been swept up in the "Zaddy" movement, a term used to describe how Pedro is the "internet's daddy." She found herself fascinated with a man she had never met. I had done a series on TikTok discussing *why* we were all like moths to a flame and she was hoping to find an answer. Rachael was a highly successful, well-known figure in the fitness industry. She had been married for the better part of two decades, had a great relationship with her two children, and lived a life many admired. She seemed to have it all together, with the only "wild hair" in her life being this pesky obsession with Mr. Pascal. That was until I asked her about her childhood.

The emotionless recount of a harrowing childhood, retold by Rachael with such ease it was as if she were discussing what she had for dinner the night before, was shocking. An absent, addicted mother who was so neglectful that twelve-year-old Rachael felt relief when she learned that she had died in a car accident. A narcissistic father whose only expression of affection was sarcastic verbal abuse dressed up as humor. Countless situations of being left alone, in danger, and with predators. Major life changes, being bullied in school, paranoia, parentification, and poverty to the point of fighting for food were just tips of the iceberg that was Rachael's childhood. Rachael felt annoyed and expressed confusion about my line of questioning. "What does any of this have to do with my weird fixation with Pedro?" she asked. With that question, we began the search for Rachael's wounded inner children. Through backtracking symptoms, Rachael began recalling childhood memories, which helped her to make tick marks on her childhood timeline. Rachael went from living in the land of DeMINDs (chapter 3) thinking her "childhood was fine" to a timeline with so many ticks she did not know where to start.

One pattern in particular began to emerge now that she could see it all on paper. No one was ever there to protect her, no one believed her, and no one kept her safe. She realized she had always longed for a safe, strong, male figure to give her shelter from the storms of life. Enter Pedro Pascal. Rachael saw that her WICs were still scared, left feeling alone, defenseless, and desperate. It was *them* looking at Pedro with longing as the father figure they never had. As Rachael began the work of reparenting her WICs, her outside world began to radically change. First, her fixation on Pedro dissipated almost overnight. Second, she opened up to her husband in a way she never had and it completely revolutionized her marriage, bringing the safety and security she had longed for. Rachael's intense paranoia, OCD tendencies, debilitating anxiety, and paralyzing insecurities melted away. She became confident, bold, empowered, and daring. Her career skyrocketed and her relationships flourished. When reflecting on her journey, Rachael captured it perfectly:

> *The signs were always there. The cries for help from my WICs, the symptoms that pointed back to unhealed wounds I had convinced myself didn't exist, my soul's desire to heal. I just didn't know what they meant or how to interpret them. I never would have thought something so silly as a celebrity crush meant something but now that I understand my WICs I love reparenting them!*

Now it is your turn. Take all that you have learned so far and begin putting pen to paper. Do not dismiss what feels silly or ignore what you don't quite understand (yet). Get curious, ask questions, take notes, and allow your WICs to begin to reveal themselves to you. Once you acknowledge them, you will see that they were there all along, trying to get your attention, even in silly or seemingly unimportant ways.

Chapter 7 Takeaways

- You can identify your WICs by using the Childhood Timeline or Backtracking Symptoms methods or whatever else comes to mind! The goal is to see our childhood on paper so that we can get a better glimpse of our WICs.

- Your WICs have always been with you, crying out for help and asking to be acknowledged. Sometimes that can present in odd ways we do not understand. By giving yourself permission to become aware, look at anything and everything, and validate it all, you will find WICs you did not know you had.

Questions to Consider

- What are some ways your WICs may have been crying out for help that you did not realize? (Examples: obsessions, phobias, addictions, chronic symptoms, fears, fantasies, and so on.)

- How do you feel sitting with your symptoms and reaching back into your childhood? It is okay to be resistant, nervous, scared, or uneasy about it! Just be honest with yourself and validate how you feel.

- How many WICs have you identified? Does that number surprise you? Overwhelm you? Confuse you? All responses are valid.

CHAPTER 8

Introductions: Getting to Know Your Wounded Inner Children

"All of us are born with many parts…[and they] are not imaginary or symbolic. They are individuals who exist as an internal family within us—and the key to health and happiness is to honor, understand, and love every part."

—Richard Schwartz, *No Bad Parts*

Now that you have done the work to identify your wounded inner children, it is time to get to know them. It is time to hear what they have to say, feel what they feel, and understand what they believe. This next step in our reparenting journey takes us from a place of looking back on our childhood, as if reviewing a movie, to placing us smack-dab in the middle of that movie. Are you ready?

If you are familiar with Internal Family Systems (IFS) and the process of working with your parts, then you might have already done some of this work. If not and you are interested in understanding parts work more thoroughly, I encourage you to read Richard Schwartz's *No Bad Parts*. In essence, IFS is an evidence-based form of psychotherapy that postulates every person is made up of parts. These parts are categorized into either protective parts (called Managers or Firefighters) or wounded parts (called Exiles). IFS brings healing and transformation by helping people to connect with their protective parts and unburden their wounded parts. These parts of us are not hypotheticals or simply aspects of ourselves. They are internal beings, with beliefs, opinions, perspectives, personalities...and wounds (Schwartz 2021). *Reparenting Your Inner Child* suggests that these parts are children—wounded inner children. They hold the memories, fears, emotions, and even physical pains of our experiences. They have their own identities, ages, likes and dislikes. They have hopes, dreams, and desires. And they have something to say.

Being bold enough to get to know them is no easy feat and sometimes we can feel resistant to do so. If you feel hesitant or resistant, that is okay. Let us not pretend that we are supposed to be excited about every aspect of the healing journey. You do not have to be jumping up for joy at the thought of connecting with the terrified four-year-old or raging teenage versions of yourself. Not every part of the healing journey is rainbows and roses. Sometimes it hurts, can feel overwhelming, or uncomfortable. Let us get comfortable with being uncomfortable. Getting comfortable with being uncomfortable means surrendering to the healing journey and honoring where you are. It involves breathing *into* the pain, experiencing the emotions you have avoided for so long, and vocalizing what is going on inside of you. Difficult to do at first, but necessary, because this process leads to deep healing, intense relief, and clarity regarding who you truly are. So take a deep breath, remind yourself that it is safe for you to "go there," and *lean in*.

Mini Bios

To properly understand a person's story, we need context. How old a person was, their perspective of a situation, and what it meant to them

Introductions: Getting to Know Your Wounded Inner Children

are vital pieces of information. When it comes to our WICs, an effective way to collect this information is to create mini biographies. Mini bios start with basic demographic information and expand into more personal details. However, you do not have to go in order. You might get tidbits of information that are seemingly "out of order" from the structure of the mini bio. As you continue spending time with your WICs, more information is often revealed that helps fill out the form. The important thing is that you are establishing yourself as a safe person for your WICs to open up to. Sometimes trust needs to be built and our WICs are slow to open up. Other times, it feels like our wounded inner children have been waiting a lifetime for us to acknowledge them and are eager to talk. Some information you might find helpful to collect for your mini bios are as follows:

WIC # 1:

Name/Nickname: Nikki

Age/Stage of Development: 6ish / Stage 4: Industry vs Inferiority

Experiences: Parents had little brother, mom had an affair, parents divorced, dad left, mom got remarried

Beliefs (about self/others): "I'm forgotten about" "Why did dad leave me?" "What's wrong with me?" She feels not good enough, alone, and unlovable.

Emotions: Fear, confusion, hurt, grief, terror, anger, rage, jealousy, inferiority, insecurity, desperation, loneliness

Fears: That her mom will hurt her, that she'll never feel safe again, that her dad will forget about her, sleeping alone, the dark, loud noises

> **Unmet Needs:** Safety and security, someone to snuggle and cuddle her, someone to play with her, a comforting bedtime routine, freedom to express in a big, childlike way
>
> **Likes/Interests:** Dancing, animals, trees, the wind, her dog, her cousin, she loves being with her grandma and in the garden the most
>
> **Desires/Hopes:** She wants to be the center of someone's attention, she hopes her dad will rescue her, she wants to live in the country with her grandma, she wants to be a dancer, she wants to be beautiful, she wants to feel like it's okay to be herself and be girly
>
> **Sense of Self Impact:** Continuity—she changed who she was around different people for approval. Coherence—I think she dissociated a lot, everything feels foggy, confusing, and hollow. Authenticity—she started trying to be something she wasn't for approval.
>
> **Additional Info/Thoughts:** This stage of development was severely impacted and it makes sense why she became so performative and focused on doing well in school. She struggled with friends, constantly sought attention, and was bullied for being a "teacher's pet" and "know it all." She tried to run away from home at maybe seven or eight. It feels foggy to think about and my heart physically aches. I think she was grieving but didn't understand and was too scared to open up so she internalized it.

This mini bio template is by no means a comprehensive list, and you can add as much detail and information as you would like. You can also leave spaces blank or skip around. If you are looking at the prompts and thinking, *I have NO idea,* do not worry! I encourage you to start writing what you *do* know. When you get to a prompt you are unsure of, take a deep breath, ask it out loud, and listen. Then write *whatever* comes to mind. It does not matter if it does not make sense or you do not understand. Write it anyway. This is an excellent practice in learning to trust yourself and in building trust with your wounded inner children.

Abstract Prompts

Mini bios are not the only way to get to know your WICs. If you are artistic, love the abstract, think in images, or enjoy being creative, then lean into that! These methods can be particularly helpful for WICs who are hard to understand or do not fully trust you yet. It can also make the process more fun and interesting. Here are some questions to help get to know your wounded inner children that are more abstract:

1. What color is my WIC or what colors would I associate with it? Why?

2. What shape represents this WIC to me? Why *that* shape?

3. Where do I feel this WIC in my body?

4. What sensations do I feel in my body when I focus on this WIC?

5. What character (from a movie or book) reminds me of this WIC? Why?

6. If this WIC were in charge of my body, what would it want to do? For example, cry, run, sleep, dance, play. Why?

7. What element (earth, wind, fire, water) or season (winter, autumn, spring, summer) reminds me of this WIC? Why is that?

8. If my WIC were an animal, what animal would it be and why?

9. If my WIC had a theme song, what song would that be?

10. If my WIC were an object, what would it be? What does that teach me about this WIC?

Apart from questions, there are also many fun and creative ways in which you can get to know your wounded inner children more intimately. Here are some ideas to get you thinking:

1. Draw or paint your WIC. Pay attention to what colors you use, shapes you draw, and other choices.

2. Create a vision board (a collection of images) that you feel represents and captures your WIC.

3. Put on a song that you feel represents or sounds like your WIC and let your body move to the music. Pay attention to how you want to move and what emotions come up.

4. Dress up like your WIC. What do you feel like wearing? How do you feel wearing it?

5. Ask your WIC what it wants to do for one hour and do it if you can. What did you learn or experience?

Any of these ideas (and whatever else you can dream up) are great ways to get to know your wounded inner children. If you feel unsure which step to take, pick whatever feels easiest. Different tools can work for different WICs. The more abstract prompts often work well for WICs who are infants or toddlers. Very young wounded inner children often lack language, and we can also lack memory of that time. Even if you know the story of what happened, remember this step is not about understanding the details of what happened to you. This step is about understanding how your wounded inner children feel and think. So if all you know is that you have a wounded inner infant who feels "gray," "heavy," scared, and alone—that is enough. Draw or paint that out as an expression. You will be surprised by what can surface from deep within the recesses of our wounds when we dare to sit and listen.

Chloe's Story

Chloe was the sweetest, kindest, most easygoing person I had ever met. She came to counseling for the same reason many of us do—anxiety. She was slow to open up and struggled to share her current fears and feelings. However, she spoke openly and with ease regarding her childhood. Her *very* traumatic childhood. Chloe had only ever known dire situations and chronic abuse, so it all seemed normal to her. As Chloe began to learn about trauma, abuse, and the concept of having wounded inner children, her "it's all good" mindset shifted to "omg it's *all* trauma." Overwhelm set in. Chloe asked, "How am I supposed to identify and get to know individual WICs when my *entire* childhood was traumatic?" Chloe could not decide if she had one giant WIC or a million little ones. Instead of trying to do mini bios on a million WICs, Chloe started with one memory that constantly lived in the corner of her mind. Allowing herself to explore that memory connected Chloe with a long-ignored WIC. That experience was emotional, sort of scary, and deeply relieving.

Once that wounded inner child had the chance to share that specific memory with Chloe, it became eager to share the other memories it was holding. For Chloe, it was not one WIC per memory; she learned she had four WICs representing different stages of her childhood. Each one held the memories and pain from all the experiences during that stage. She began by assigning colors and shapes to them as that felt safer, but pretty soon she was filling out the mini bios. Feeling comfortable expressing emotions artistically, Chloe took the information from the mini bios she had collected and painted one WIC, sculpted another, wrote a poem for the third, and created an image board for the fourth. It was beautiful, liberating, healing, and surprisingly fun. What started as feeling overwhelming and confusing became an exciting journey of self-discovery. Chloe and her WICs celebrated together.

So get your party hat on. Your WICs are waiting.

Chapter 8 Takeaways

- Your wounded inner children are real-life beings inside of you who hold memories, emotions, and pain. They have fears, hopes, and beliefs. Getting to know them helps in healing them.

- Get creative, lean into your gifts, and use whatever structure you would like to get to know your WICs. Choose what feels easiest and most relieving.

- We can have many WICs and often we continue to discover them over time. Start with what you feel ready for and allow the process to unfold organically. There is no rush.

Questions to Consider

- Is there a wounded inner child who is at the forefront of your mind, trying to get your attention, that you feel drawn toward? If so, trust it and start there.

- What ways of getting to know your WICs feel easiest, most relieving, or exciting? Dive in!

- What emotions, fears, or concerns rise up within you when you contemplate that getting to know your WICs is a messy process with no right way or wrong answers? Sometimes coming to terms with this fact can be difficult and we can doubt ourselves. Give yourself permission to feel however you feel and validate it!

Reparenting

SECTION 3

CHAPTER 9

Parenting Styles: How Were You Raised?

You have taken the time to listen to and connect with your WICs. You have learned who they are, their interests, hopes, and fears. Like with any relationship, you are steadily building trust and deepening your connection with them. But before you can begin reparenting them, you must first understand one crucial truth so that you do not further wound your WICs or perpetuate cycles of abuse. This truth, which we are going to unpack, often gets overlooked in the reparenting journey, and without knowing this information, many people end up feeling exhausted while also feeling discouraged that reparenting does not seem to be working.

You see, as adults we are often able to look back on our childhoods and understand what happened, what hurt us, and how it impacted us—from a logical standpoint. We can *logically* comprehend that being yelled at constantly made us timid and conflict resistant. We can *logically* grasp that berating, criticizing, or belittling a child is wrong. It makes *logical* sense to us that if we were kinder and more self-compassionate, we may feel some relief from our pain. We then try to apply that logic to our healing journey but see little progress. We get frustrated and discouraged because *logically* we do not understand why it is not working. That is because *logic* has nothing to do with it. It has everything to do with our *programming*. Our programming is the crucial truth of our childhood that we need to understand in order to not get stuck.

Reflect on these questions. Are you always there for your loved ones? Do you lend an ear for listening and a shoulder to cry on without being asked twice? Are you there with a kind word, a compassionate smile, and a warm hug for anyone who needs it? If you said yes to any of these questions, the next question to answer is—do you treat yourself the same way? What about when *you* need an ear, a shoulder, or a smile? Do you share how you feel, reach out for help, and ask for support because you know you deserve it and believe others care? Or do you feel like a burden to others when talking about your problems? Are you embarrassed and ashamed when showing emotion? Do you put everything and everyone before yourself? If you find that you tend to treat others differently (better) than you treat yourself, I want you to remember this saying:

How we treat others is a reflection of our character. How we treat ourselves is a reflection of our programming.

Programming, essentially, is how we were parented. How our caregivers treated us has a way of becoming the blueprint for how we treat ourselves. Sometimes that can extend into the ways we treat others (especially when we were younger), but as we age the gap can widen. You might find yourself the doting mother, the caring friend, the supportive coworker. Patient, kind, and loving…with everyone but yourself. Maybe you have tried to treat yourself better, but it never seems to stick. That is often because, while our intentions are good, we end up reparenting ourselves with the same parental programming that wounded us. That is what this chapter is for. We are going to walk through the four different parenting styles, how they manifest, and the impact they have on us. This information deepens our understanding of the wounds our inner child or children holds and how to reparent our WICs in a way that heals those wounds, not perpetuates them. An accompanying worksheet can be found online.

Parenting Styles

The concept of parenting styles was first introduced by Diana Baumrind in the 1970s, when she presented three categories to describe typical parenting behaviors. Eleanor Maccoby and John Martin introduced a fourth style in the 1980s, which Baumrind ended up including as well (Kuppens and Ceulemans 2019). As we go through each of the four styles, there are a few things to keep in mind. First, it is important to recognize that cultural influences, socioeconomic status, and a parent's upbringing all influence a caregiver's parenting style. Second, caregivers can have a blended approach to parenting styles. Lastly, parenting styles can change over time and among children. Gabor Maté, a Canadian physician and leading expert on childhood trauma, addiction, and the impacts of stress, discusses how no two children, even within the same family unit, have the same experiences or even upbringing (Maté and Maté 2022). Changes in age, maturity level of the parents, practice as a caregiver, changes in life and lifestyle, and increased or decreased access to resources, education, and support are just some of the factors that contribute to how and why siblings experience a different version of the same caregiver. If you feel you were treated differently than your siblings, or experienced changes in how you were parented over the course of your childhood, keep this in mind as we go through the four parenting styles: permissive, uninvolved/neglectful, authoritarian, and authoritative. An article written by Terrence Sanvictores and Magda Mendez, published by the National Library of Medicine in 2022, summarizes them well; let's explore.

Permissive

The permissive parenting style is often loving and nurturing with open communication between parent and child. It also has very few rules and little to no expectations, which lends itself to little discipline or punishment. The parent interacts with the child as more of a friend than a caregiver, which in turn provides space for the child to be able to solve problems on their own. Which can be helpful and harmful. This parenting style has both positive and negative outcomes. Children of permissive parents tend to have higher levels of self-esteem and moderate social skills. But they also tend to suffer from unhealthy eating habits, poor bedtime routines (which can interrupt sleep and therefore development), too much screen time, and issues with homework. This can lead to health problems and issues with structure and routine later in life. Children of permissive parents also tend to be selfish, impulsive, demanding, and cannot self-regulate. Regina George's mother in the movie *Mean Girls* is an example of a permissive parent.

Uninvolved/Neglectful

Parents who are uninvolved or neglectful fall on a spectrum of severity regarding neglect. In most cases, they still meet the basic needs of their child (food, clothing, shelter) but remain detached and emotionally absent. They give their children almost endless freedom, have no expectations, and provide limited communication. There is no set style of discipline and correction can be impulsive, random, and range from fair to punitive. The outcomes of this parenting style have more cons than pros. The children tend to be resilient and self-sufficient but out of necessity rather than as a fostered virtue. They have trouble controlling their emotions and have academic challenges, poor coping skills, and difficulty nurturing and maintaining healthy relationships. The parents of Mike and Nancy Wheeler in *Stranger Things* are examples of uninvolved/neglectful parents.

Authoritarian

Authoritarian parents live up to their name. They parent with an iron fist, so to speak. There is a one-way style of communication ("I talk, you listen") and total compliance and perfect obedience are demanded. They institute strict rules, which are often not explained to the child, and there is little room for error. They tend to punish their children instead of discipline, and there is often little to no affection. The outcome of this parenting style is deceiving at first. Children of authoritarian parents are good at adhering to instructions and meeting goals. They are often the most well-behaved and obedient children...for a while. But because their behavior stems from fear of punishment, it lasts only as long as the threat of punishment is there. The children often rebel as they get older and have higher levels of aggression and difficulty managing their anger. While they are good at performing and meeting the demands of others, they tend to be shy, socially inept, struggle to make decisions, and have very poor self-esteem. Lucius Malfoy, the father of Draco Malfoy in the *Harry Potter* series, is an example of an authoritarian parent.

Authoritative

Authoritative, while sounding similar to authoritarian, is almost the exact opposite. Authoritative parents are driven first and foremost by their relationship with their child. The priority is nurturing a close and safe relationship with their child built on mutual respect and trust. They present clear guidelines for the child and have frequent and open communication about boundaries, rules, and consequences. Authoritative parents do not punish their children (meaning they focus on imputing consequences for the offense) but rather provide discipline (meaning they focus on respectful and safe strategies to help their children grow and develop) while maintaining a strong bond. Their children have a voice and are encouraged to provide input and share their perspectives. This parenting style is the most difficult to execute as it requires patience, self-awareness, emotional intelligence, maturity, and tremendous effort. However, the outcomes of this style make the effort it takes worth it. Children of this style are confident, responsible, independent, and have high self-esteem. As they grow, they learn to manage negative emotions in healthy ways, regulate themselves, accomplish their goals, and tend to have higher levels of academic achievement. The newest term for this style of parenting is called "gentle parenting." Mufasa in *The Lion King* is an example of this parenting style.

Parenting Style and Reparenting

Understanding the different parenting styles provides us with a new lens through which we can look back on our childhood, giving us clarity and meaning to the ways our parents treated us. It can also help us reflect on why we are the way we are now. So what do parenting styles have to do with reparenting? To answer that question we have to first understand that the parenting style our caregivers used when we were children is often how we continue to treat ourselves now. We sometimes fail to make this connection because how we treat others can be the exact opposite of how our parents treated us. Maybe your parents were emotionally neglectful and selfish, so you vowed to never be like them. Now as an adult you consistently put others before yourself, tend to their needs, and are always available. But do *you* count as one of those people you treat that way? Remember, how we treat *others* is often a reflection of our *character*. But more often than not, we are not treating ourselves the same way. That is because how we treat *ourselves* is often a reflection of our *programming*—the way we were parented. And because we subconsciously continue to treat (parent) ourselves the way our caregivers did, we also tend to respond to the cries of our wounded inner children in the same manner. We are subconsciously treating our WICs in the very same manner that caused their wounds to begin with, and we do not even realize it. This perpetuates the cycle of pain, broken trust, and self-abuse within us. To help our WICs and heal our wounds, we must parent them in a new way; we must re-parent them. *This* is why reparenting ourselves and our wounded inner children is so vital to our quality of life, happiness, and health. As you embark on your reparenting journey, an important step is to commit to breaking the parenting-style cycle within you and to reparent your WICs in a manner and style they needed then and that you need now. Are you ready to make that commitment?

Kal's Story

Kal had been working on reparenting themselves for years. Due to the level and severity of childhood trauma, it had been slow and steady going. Kal worked through childhood sexual abuse, physical abuse, neglect, household dysfunction, and sibling trauma. With each wound that they healed they felt a little more steady, stable, and sane. But there was one wound in particular that seemed to have them in its grip and they just could not shake loose no matter how hard they tried. Kal was raised in an extremely religious household, which lent itself to an authoritarian parenting style by both parents. Growing up, there was never any thought for how they felt and there was no room to develop an opinion (let alone a personality), as children were to be seen and not heard, obey their parents, and put everyone before themselves. Kal's programming was to reject who they were and hate themselves for their very nature was "evil." Kal did the best they could, but it was never enough, and shame became their default setting. Kal had worked through the pain their parents caused them; however, they still suffered greatly in day-to-day life with self-hate and doubt, people pleasing, and codependency. It was not until Kal learned about parenting styles that the dots connected. They had been *trying* to reparent themselves but were doing so with the same parenting-style programming as their parents. Learning about the different styles empowered Kal to practice building skills they had never seen modeled. Patience, kindness, compassion, understanding, support, and acceptance, just to name a few. As they honed these skills and chose to *only* engage with their WICs when they were in the headspace to be a gentle parent, they became unstuck and finally felt movement in areas they had been struggling with for years.

Chapter 9 Takeaways

- There are four parenting styles: uninvolved/neglectful, permissive, authoritarian, and authoritative (gentle).

- Parenting styles can be a blend, change over time, and are influenced by several factors.

- Committing to re-programming ourselves allows us to reparent our wounded inner children in the way they need.

Questions to Consider

- Which parenting style(s) were you raised with? How do you know?

- How did that parenting style impact you both as a child and now as an adult?

- What style do your WICs need? What style do you need? Write it out!

CHAPTER 10

Reparenting: In the Here and Now

Let the reparenting part of your healing journey begin! You have done the work to identify your wounds and understand how they came to be. Now it is time to begin healing them, by reparenting yourself. There are two approaches you can take to reparent yourself—in the here and now and with your wounded inner children. We will look at reparenting your WICs in the next chapter. For now, we are going to look at how to put together a plan to reparent yourself *now* and why that is important. Reparenting in the here and now means reparenting the adult you are now and not specifically your WICs. Remember there is no set order or hard and fast rules. You can reparent yourself in whatever way feels best for you. However, many people feel trepidatious about reparenting their WICs first. So starting with reparenting yourself in the here and now can be a great way to ease into the process. This is also a great option if you want to change habits or see improvements in your current lifestyle.

Parenting Passed Down

Reparenting who you are *now* requires that you understand how you were parented and how you are perpetuating that type of parental treatment toward yourself. Remember from the previous chapter that how you were parented often becomes your programming for how you treat yourself. We are going to call the perpetuation of treating yourself the way your parents treated you "parenting passed down" (PPD). This cycle can continue past how you treat yourself and move down the generational line to the way you parent your children. Even the most resolute person who determines not to treat themselves and others in the same ways their parents treated them still has to do the work if they want to successfully break the cycle. Reparenting yourself in the here and now empowers you to do this work intentionally. With the awareness of how your caregivers parented you, an understanding of your programming, and the tools to create change, you will effectively break generational cycles of trauma and abuse and experience healing and relief. A good place to start is to get a clear understanding of at least three areas in your life where you are perpetuating the PPD cycle. The most common areas are:

- The beliefs we hold about ourselves (our worth, value, purpose)
- The relationship we have with our emotions
- The way we talk to ourselves (often our inner critic)
- The way we treat ourselves when we make a mistake, struggle, or fail

Take time to think about how your parents handled these areas when raising you. If you are struggling, some questions to ask yourself are:

- What messages about my worth, value, and purpose did I receive from my parents? (This can be verbally and nonverbally.)
- How did my parents treat my emotions? What was I taught about emotions?

- How did my parents talk to me and about me? Are there any criticisms from my parents that I still carry?

- How did my parents treat me when I made mistakes, struggled, or failed at something? What was the message I received about my shortcomings?

If you want to go more in depth, use the Parenting Passed Down worksheet in the free materials online as a guide.

Reparenting Yourself

Once you have identified ways in which you are continuing to treat yourself in the same manner your parents did, it is time to work through the reparenting steps. You are not focusing on how your parents *could* have treated you (and the difference that might have made), as that is in the next chapter. Instead, you are going to focus on how you could begin treating yourself differently *now*. To do that you are going to follow four reparenting steps:

1. Identify your PPD (which you have just done using the questions in the previous section or the worksheet in the free materials)

2. Examine how treating yourself in these ways makes you feel and impacts your quality of life

3. Describe in detail how you could reparent yourself (treat yourself differently than what you were taught)

4. Predict how reparenting yourself in this way could impact you

5. Reparent yourself. Practice your new programming, treating yourself in these new ways

Let's look briefly at steps two through four so that you have a thorough understanding of what they entail and how to execute them successfully.

Step two (examining how we treat ourselves) requires that you get in touch with your emotions. That might sound simple, but it is a struggle for many. If you were raised by an emotionally immature parent or emotions were not discussed, then you likely did not develop the skills to be able to identify and label what you were experiencing internally. We do not become emotionally mature simply because we age. It takes being intentional to develop a relationship with your emotions. This is not a step you can skip. It also is not one you should be ashamed of. A lot of us were raised during times when emotions were disregarded, or it might have been socially or culturally taboo to discuss or express emotions. Learning to identify and connect with your emotions is a form of reparenting in and of itself that can be deeply healing. If you struggle to find the words for what you are experiencing, you can use a feelings wheel. Do a quick online search and you will find thousands to pick from. Aim to identify three emotions that you experience when you treat yourself in the same manner that your parents did.

Step three (how to reparent yourself) is tricky because it can look simple on paper, but executing it often is not. For many of the PPD cycles we are caught in, identifying the opposite of what our parents did is a great place to start. For example, if you were treated like you did not matter and you still tell yourself that you do not matter, the obvious reparenting approach would be to tell yourself that you *do* matter. However, when we introduce a statement that directly opposes our beliefs, we can experience a visceral reaction of rejection or recoil. New statements or ways of treating yourself will not match what you have been doing and what you believe, so it feels wrong and like a lie. Sometimes speaking to ourselves more lovingly and compassionately can cause our skin to crawl. However, that does not mean it *is* wrong, a lie, or not worth doing. The compulsion to reject a new way of treating yourself is a built-in form of self-defense aimed to protect you.

Often to protect you from emotions you might be scared to feel. Your mind might be flooded with objections and what-ifs. *If I'm kind to myself, I will not try as hard; If I ignore my shortcomings, I will not improve.* These thoughts are the voices of your old programming fighting to stay in power. Confronting these thoughts and committing to reparenting yourself will help silence those voices more quickly. Believing something new about yourself might be uncomfortable at first, but it is nowhere near as painful as continuing to believe as you have. Daring to break free from your programming, standing up to the voices within, and learning to treat yourself in a kinder, more loving way will change your life. Be kind to yourself as you work through this step and recognize that there may be a gap between identifying what you need to reparent yourself and being able to do it. But keep going, because you *will* get there.

Step four (predicting reparenting impact) empowers you to persevere and can help you work through the previous steps if you feel stuck. In this step, you will imagine a future you who has mastered reparenting yourself in the areas you want to focus on. Envision yourself treating yourself the way you want to. For example, maybe every time you look at yourself you criticize yourself, which is a behavior you learned from your mother. Now imagine a future you, looking exactly as you do now, standing in front of the mirror. You smile kindly at yourself, admiring your unique features that make you distinctly you. You feel gratitude and love for your body and all that it has done for you. You roll your shoulders back, put your chin up, and say to yourself, *I love myself as I am*. How will treating yourself that way cause you to feel? What impact could treating yourself that way have on your life? What emotions come up for you during this exercise? Write them down. Get as specific as you can. If objections arise, explore where they are coming from and why you have them. But do *not* agree with them or let them take back over. Our brain does not like change and sometimes it can feel scarier to have hope than it is to stay stuck, but that does not mean it is more dangerous. It feeling scary does not mean that you should not try. You deserve healing, you deserve freedom, you deserve love.

Practice Makes for Reparented

Write down your responses to each of the steps so you can see exactly what you need to do. Writing provides you with some accountability as well as clarity. Sometimes when dealing with our wounds we can forget, lose sight of what we are doing, or want to quit. All of that is normal. In a later chapter, we will look at how to make a reparenting plan to help you get organized. If you have a safe person in your life, tell them about the areas you are focusing on reparenting in your life so that they can encourage you, hold you accountable if necessary, and celebrate with you as you make progress.

Reparenting in the here and now is not something that is accomplished quickly. It took years, maybe even decades, for you to establish the way you currently treat yourself, and it is going to take some time to change that. Give yourself time to try it out and practice this new way of being before moving on to reparenting your wounded inner children. Take a week to try out reparenting yourself in a chosen area. Get a feel for how hard or easy it is and work through any emotions that come up. Practice creating reminders or setting aside time to reparent yourself as it takes time and focus to create a new habit. It does not matter how long it takes; what matters is that you get started, keep going, and do not quit!

Riley's Story

Riley had a relentlessly abusive inner critic. It did not matter what Riley did, her thoughts toward herself were always hypercritical and fault finding. But the real problem was that Riley did not see this as an issue. Her thoughts did not *feel* critical; they felt *true* because this view of herself was all she had ever known. When Riley attempted to explore how these thoughts made her feel, her brain shut it down immediately because she had been taught emotions did not matter. Riley was stuck in a parenting-passed-down loop and could not find a way out—until she began working the steps.

It was not a battle easily won. Riley fought tooth and nail for her healing. Step one was met with constant justification of her parents' actions and why their verbal abuse was warranted because it was "accurate." Step two had to be skipped because Riley could not yet access her emotions. Step three took time because, even though Riley could think of other ways to treat herself, she argued why it was a bad idea to try. It would make her weak, make her lazy, she would be lying to herself, she did not deserve a break. Step four was where she finally felt something give. It was hard for Riley to entertain the idea of treating herself differently, but when she did, everything shifted. Riley started with a very simple reparenting approach that was wildly effective. Using alarms and sticky notes designed to catch her attention, ten times a day, every day for a week, Riley would stop and say out loud, "I am doing the best I can." That's it. But that simple statement flew directly in the face of her parental programming and against everything she felt was true.

Riley initially agreed to the challenge of saying the statement out loud because it seemed simple enough and she did not have much faith it would work. But when it came time to actually reparent herself and say "I am doing the best I can" out loud, she found herself unable to. Like, physically unable to speak the words. The first time she finally squeaked out the words she burst into tears. By the second day, she was crying freely. By the end of the week, she felt tremendous physical relief and was sleeping better than she had in years. Riley realized that not only was it true (she *was* doing the best she could), but being more compassionate with herself empowered her to do even better. Riley had broken a generational cycle of criticism and experienced the profound freedom of reparenting by saying seven simple words.

Chapter 10 Takeaways

- We often treat ourselves the same way our parents did and that can perpetuate cycles of abuse causing continued suffering.

- Reparenting yourself in the here and now is an effective way to break habits, create change, and experience healing.

- The four steps provide you with an outline to use on how to reparent yourself in the here and now. You do not have to go in order and you can take your time as needed.

Questions to Consider

- What three areas of your life are you still parenting yourself in the same manner your caregivers parented you?

- What step do you feel most nervous or unsure about? Why do you think that is?

- What are you most excited about experiencing when it comes to reparenting yourself in the here and now?

CHAPTER 11

Reparenting: Your WICs

Your wounded inner children have waited patiently as you have cultivated the understanding, safety, and compassion needed to reparent them. What you do not realize is that, in doing so, you have already begun the reparenting journey. You have invested time in meeting your WICs by exploring aspects of yourself you previously resisted. You learned about who they are, how they were hurt, and their perspectives by diving into the depths of your childhood in a way many are too afraid to do. You have held space for them, built trust, and listened to them with each emotion you have allowed yourself to feel. That is self-love and the foundation of reparenting. The goal is to keep moving forward and help them release their burdens, heal their hurts, and set them free. Free to either grow up (like some of them will choose to do) or free to engage in the wonders of childhood, unrestrained from the trauma that bound them.

In the previous chapter, you learned how to reparent yourself in the here and now by creating a practical plan you can institute into your day-to-day life. Given that the wounds of your WICs live in the past, reparenting them requires a different approach. There are countless ways to reparent your wounded inner children, and you are encouraged to follow what feels right; however, in this chapter, we will explore five reparenting exercises. Then in the next chapter, we will look at how to create a reparenting plan for your reparenting journey so that you can learn how to prioritize and implement reparenting into your life in a sustainable and measurable way.

Reparenting Exercises

The five reparenting exercises we are going to examine are:

- Talk It Out
- Act It Out
- Play the Movie
- Empty Chair
- WIC-Led Action

Talk It Out

This reparenting method is a continuation of what you did when you initially got to know your WICs in chapter 8. It is a back-and-forth dialogue between you and your WIC regarding their experiences, wounds, fears, and needs. This is a great method for WICs who are above age five, have memories of experiences, and trust you. For this exercise:

- Speak out loud (if you are able and comfortable).
- Record yourself or take notes so you can revisit or remember the conversation.
- Ask age-appropriate questions using age-appropriate language just as you would if you were speaking with a child that is the age of your WIC.

- Trust, without hesitation, the initial response to your questions from your WIC. This often comes in the form of a small inner voice, fleeting thought, or visual in your mind's eye.

- If answers are slow to come, fret not. Remain calm, focus on your breath, and allow for awkward silence. If you get the feeling your WIC does not know or does not want to respond, honor that just like you would if you were talking to another human. This is self-respect and grows trust between you and your WIC.

- You might feel silly or uncomfortable. It can feel odd talking to yourself at first, but that does not mean there is anything wrong with it. It is okay to be uncomfortable, just keep going!

Example: Every week you spend fifteen minutes talking to your thirteen-year-old WIC. At first, you get to know them. Then you talk through what they experienced and how it made them feel. Maybe you cry together or rage together. You validate their pain and hold space for their hurt. Then you begin discussing their hopes, fears, and needs to move forward. Maybe they finally feel heard and have hope they will feel better. Or they express feeling uncertain about who they are and need your help and support as they explore their likes and dislikes. Throughout this process, your WIC is healing, you are feeling relief from the weight of the pain you have carried, and you are developing aspects of your sense of self—you are growing up!

Act It Out

In Van der Kolk's best seller *The Body Keeps the Score*, he discusses the powerful impact psychodrama has on healing trauma (2015). Psychodrama is re-enacting experiences, memories, or past events in a way that is cathartic and healing. It is effective because the brain does not understand that it is pretending or acting, and so it allows us to reconnect to an experience we need to heal from in a safe way. In reparenting your WICs, you can do this one of two ways. You can elicit the help of other safe people to act out a scene with you, or you can do it on your own. The most important thing to understand is that you are *not* acting out what *happened*. You are acting out what you *needed* or *wanted* to happen in a way that brings healing. If you are working with others, assume the role of your WIC and assign others to the roles of your caregivers. If you are doing it alone, externally you are the parent while the WIC is responding from within you. For this exercise:

- Pick one specific scenario from your childhood at a time.

- For every interaction within that scenario that hurt your WIC, reparent them by re-enacting how they wanted or needed their caregiver to respond.

- Feeling awkward, uncomfortable, and vulnerable is part of why it is so effective, so feeling this way is okay!

- This exercise can be very emotional. Make sure you have a safe space, time to process, and coping skills that help you.

Example:

The scenario: When you were eight you fell off your bike and scraped your knees. You ran to your parent, crying. They laughed at you, called you a baby, and told you to toughen up. You went to your room to hide your crying, feeling alone with your knees throbbing.

Acting it out with someone: You play eight-year-old you and your best friend plays your parent. You recall the scenario and allow the emotion and pain of your WIC to rise. You go to your friend just as you did your parent. They hold and comfort you, putting a cold washcloth on your knees and your favorite bandages (bonus if they are kid ones). They tell you they are proud of you, that it is okay to cry, and they will sit with you as long as you need. You stay in that moment until you feel comfort and relief.

Acting it out alone: You recall the scenario and allow the emotion to rise. You, acting as the parent, hug yourself. You tend to your knees and speak out loud to your WIC, telling them all the things they need to hear. You physically ice your knees and put bandages on them. You allow your WIC to cry while you validate their pain and fear for as long as they need until you feel comfort and relief.

Play the Movie

This exercise is effective for people who like to daydream or use their imagination to visualize. The goal of this exercise is to rewrite history by directing a new ending to an old movie (memory). Start by picking a memory of a situation that your WIC was wounded by. Now imagine watching it like a movie in your mind's eye. Imagine you are the director directing the scene and on standby is the hero of the movie. That hero is Adult You as you exist now. Pick a point, or several, within the movie to yell, "Cut!" and direct your hero to jump in. Watch as Adult You steps into the memory and intercedes. Let this memory play out in a new way, with an alternate ending, where Adult You rescues, removes, protects, defends, or comforts your WIC. Observe your WIC's response. What are they feeling? How do they react? What do they say? Emotions of relief, hope, comfort, and expressed grief are signs of effective reparenting. This exercise bonds you and your WIC, builds confidence, trust, and safety within, and teaches your WICs that they are no longer alone. You are there for them. Past present, and future. You will keep them safe. Keep in mind:

- This is an emotional exercise because you are giving your WIC what they did not get. This can connect you to the pain of what was, the grief of what was not, and the emotions of your WIC getting what they need now.

- You may have to play a specific movie (memory) multiple times and your endings might change. Sometimes we can only do a little at a time, and since you are new to reparenting you may try one thing, only to learn your WIC needs something else. Honoring that is reparenting too!

- Narrating the movie out loud is particularly helpful in being able to stay present, stay focused, and connect more deeply to your emotions.

- If you are going to use this exercise for several memories, write out or record your movies to avoid confusion or forgetting.

Example: You replay the movie of four-year-old you being yelled at for breaking something even though it was an accident. You watch as your parent bellows at your WIC, swats them, and then sends them to their room. You see your WIC sobbing into the pillow so no one would hear, feeling a range of intense and confusing emotions, and the longing for comfort. You yell, "Cut!" and you send Adult You (equipped with all the love, compassion, power, and protectiveness needed) to the front door of your childhood home. You yell, "Action!" and watch as Adult You bursts through the front door, startling your parent. Adult You confronts them, saying, "How DARE you treat a child, *your* child, that way! Don't you EVER raise your voice at them or put your hands on them again, do you understand me?!" Your caregiver apologizes and nods silently in embarrassment. Adult You storms off toward your childhood bedroom, knocking gently before opening the door. Adult You sits calmly on the end of your WIC's bed. Your wounded inner child peeks out from the covers they are crying under. Adult You tells your WIC how sorry you are that they were treated so poorly, that they do not deserve that, and that you understand how they feel. You watch as your WIC flies out of bed and jumps into your arms. Adult You holds and rocks your WIC as they sob out all their emotions while Adult You is regulated, calm, and safe. Adult You tells your WIC how much you love them and how you will always protect them. When the emotions have ebbed and the relief has washed over you, you conclude the scene.

Empty Chair

The empty chair exercise is a commonly used technique in therapy. It was introduced over a hundred years ago by Jacob Levy Moreno, a student of Sigmund Freud, but it was popularized in the 1950s by Fitz Perls, the founder of Gestalt therapy (Mann 2021). While the therapeutic applications of this method can be complex and multifaceted, the premise is simple. Put a chair in front of you, imagine a person in it, and then speak to them. There are dozens of ways this exercise has been adapted to help people with all sorts of struggles and it is a great tool for reparenting. There are a few ways to do this:

- Imagine your WIC in the chair
- Imagine your parent in the chair and speak to them as your WIC
- Imagine your parent in the chair and speak to them as yourself now on behalf of your WIC

The intention is to address either the wounder or the wounded from a place of safety. Depending on which option you choose, the goals are to:

- Connect with and express the emotions of your wounded inner child
- Say all the things you or your WIC need to say to the parent who hurt you
- Feel empowered by confronting the parent and advocating for yourself and your WIC

You can pick a specific instance or you can address the person as a whole. This is not merely a mental exercise. You need a real chair, to sit across from it, and to speak out loud what you need to say to whomever you have imagined is sitting there.

Example as your WIC: You sit across from an empty chair and imagine your mother sitting in it. You address her as your sixteen-year-old WIC. You express your confusion, hurt, and anger at the way she treats you, allowing yourself to cry and raise your voice. You say out loud what you have never said before. You give your WIC the space and time needed to express it all and conclude when you feel relief or feel that your WIC is finished.

WIC-Led Action

This reparenting exercise sometimes comes after you have done the other exercises to reparent specific wounds. But it can also be used in the beginning to connect with WICs who do not trust you or are hesitant to open up. This exercise is similar to what we see in play therapy or child-led play. The goal is to allow your WICs the opportunity to express their needs and have opportunities to engage with you, or the world, how they would like. There are an infinite number of WIC-led actions, but the most common are:

- Your WIC wants to play (to dance, sing, play with toys, play at a playground)

- Your WIC wants comfort (a hug, to be rocked, sung to, a bath, a stuffed animal)

- Your WIC wants to experience something specific (swimming at a lake, getting ice cream, going to the zoo, watching a movie)

- Your WIC wants to express how they feel in a way that feels comfortable (by drawing a picture, coloring, acting it out, telling a story with toys, crying)

WIC-led action is deeply liberating and healing. Our WICs get to experience being a child in ways they were denied or robbed of. But we can sometimes feel silly or embarrassed doing this reparenting exercise. That is okay. Be patient with yourself; honor what you are comfortable with and feel ready for. This exercise is one that often allows WICs who would like to grow up to begin that process.

Lisa's Story

Lisa did everything she could to forget her childhood and separate herself from her WICs. But when her symptoms became unmanageable and the nightmares overwhelming, she turned to reparenting. The exercises sounded too daunting and vulnerable at first, so she picked WIC-led action despite feeling foolish and insecure. Once a week for thirty minutes she picked a WIC she had identified and asked them what they wanted to do (within the comfort of her own home). In the beginning, she found herself watching movies from her childhood, coloring, baking brownies, taking naps, and having dance parties in her living room. As she got more comfortable she ventured out of her home. She went on walks, jumped in puddles, swung on swings, and skipped rocks. Then one day when she asked her WIC what they wanted to do, they replied, "Talk about what happened." That led Lisa into the next step of her reparenting journey: talking it out. She was scared it was going to be a long and arduous process, but she was surprised to see that once her WIC had been able to share their experience and how they felt, had a good cry, and received comfort from Lisa (she did lots of self-hugs and rocking), the sting of the painful memory eased, Lisa's symptoms decreased, and her WIC went back to wanting to play. Lisa learned that reparenting her WICs, while vulnerable and sometimes emotional, was not nearly as hard to do as carrying around the pain of her unhealed WICs.

Chapter 11 Takeaways

- There are infinite ways to reparent your WICs and you are encouraged to trust yourself, listen to your WICs, and choose what you feel ready for.

- Five helpful reparenting exercises you can use to get you started are: talking it out, acting it out, play the movie, empty chair, and WIC-led action.

- It is normal to feel a little awkward, uncomfortable, vulnerable, or emotional at first. Be kind to yourself and be patient with your WICs.

Questions to Consider

- Which of the five reparenting exercises intrigued you the most? Why do you think that is?

- Which of the five reparenting exercises seems the scariest? Why do you think that is?

- What are five ways in which you feel you would benefit from reparenting your WICs? Write them down!

CHAPTER 12

Reparenting Plan: Staying Consistent to See Success

In the previous chapter, you examined five key exercises for reparenting your WICs. You learned how and why to do them and asked yourself some honest questions about taking this step. However, before diving in, there are some important concepts to understand as well as structure that needs to be created so that you can create long-lasting, sustainable success. This is done with the use of a reparenting plan. A reparenting plan is a game plan of sorts that allows you to take into consideration your needs, your lifestyle, and your concerns by creating a written contract. You can use this reparenting plan to hold yourself accountable for doing the work to reparent your WICs and yourself in the here and now. Let us look at some of the things you need to know before creating your reparenting plan.

First, reparenting your wounded inner children takes time, dedication, and consistency. While many people experience relief, healing, or change as soon as the first exercise, this is not a one-and-done situation. Think of a child who goes through a traumatic situation. They need to process through it by talking about it and that might take multiple conversations. But that is not all they need. They will have residual symptoms (and trauma responses) that require a safe person they can seek repeatedly for comfort, reassurance, and regulation, as many times as they need until they can release it. After that, they still need a parent, a family, a place of belonging. It is important to recognize that reparenting your WICs includes all of this and is often a lifelong relationship that requires your commitment.

Second, reparenting your wounded inner children needs to be prioritized within your schedule. The initial reparenting exercises, designed to help your WICs with their wounds, require that time be set aside to do so. This is not something you are going to want to do during your lunch break. These exercises take time and require a level of safety so that you can allow yourself to be vulnerable, as emotions tend to arise as you work through the exercises. While there is no requirement on how often or frequently you need to reparent, it is encouraged that you commit to include reparenting into your life with some consistency in the beginning. We all have busy lives and if we do not intentionally prioritize reparenting, we are not likely to do it. Especially because your brain is not exactly excited about you connecting to something painful. Whether you reparent once a day, week, or month, do what works best for you, but *do* pencil it in. Aim to set aside at least thirty minutes during a time when you will have no distractions and where you feel safe and comfortable.

Lastly, when it comes to where to start, or with whom—trust yourself. Some people choose to start with a WIC that feels less burdened or wounded as that feels less daunting or scary. Some people choose to start with the WIC who is always the first in their mind, the one that they cannot stop thinking about. Some choose to start with the most wounded, or the "original" WIC, as that can create a domino effect for healing other wounded inner children who are closely tied to or are a result of that "original" WIC. What is most important in deciding where to start is honoring what you feel ready for and where you *want* to start. You are also allowed to change your mind. You may realize that crafting this reparenting plan feels like too much too soon—that is okay. Start smaller or with what feels doable. Or maybe you are a ways into reparenting one WIC and you realize it would be more beneficial to address a different WIC first before continuing and you are not sure what to do. Trust yourself, follow what feels best, and allow the process to be messy. All of these reactions, emotions, and change-ups are okay! There are no hard and fast rules in reparenting your wounded inner children, and allowing yourself the freedom to follow your heart is a great exercise in trusting yourself, honoring your needs, and protecting yourself from unnecessary stress or harm. Which, as you have learned, is a way to reparent yourself in the here and now. It's a win-win!

Reparenting Plan

Once you have decided how often you would like to practice reparenting, mark it off in your calendar. Schedule it like an appointment. Let's say your goal is once a week for thirty minutes on Sunday morning. Next, collect all of your information regarding your WIC and your plan for reparenting them into one place. This is where the reparenting plan comes in. There is a Reparenting Plan template available in the free resources to use as a guide. For each wounded inner child, fill out the following:

- The wound or issue (the problem you have identified)
- WIC (the wounded inner child connected to this wound or issue)
- Parenting programming (how you still treat yourself or your WIC based on how you were raised)
- Reparenting plan (the action you are going to take to reparent your WIC and yourself in the here and now)

Here is an example of what a reparenting plan can look like:

- **Wound/Issue:** *Abandoned/rejected by father several times throughout life. This has caused low self-esteem, seeking male attention for approval, being inauthentic, and feeling unlovable.*

- **WIC:** *Name: Nikki. Age: 14. She is angry, confused, mistrusting, hates men but craves their attention and approval, and she feels lost.*

- **Parenting Programming:** *I judge myself, feel shame, and hate myself for being this way. I say to myself things my parents said to me, like "I am boy crazy" and "a slut with no standards." I have ignored the cries of this WIC for a long time and I tell her to "just grow up" when she is upset.*

- **Reparenting Plan:** *I am going to practice kinder self-talk to myself and my WIC. I will spend thirty minutes every week journaling about my WIC's hurts, fears, experiences, and hopes until I feel like I understand her better and our relationship has improved. When I am ready I am going to do the Play the Movie exercise and give her all the love, support, and safety she needs to heal. My goal is to be the safe, accepting mother she needs to work through this wound as a teenager.*

Once you have your reparenting plan created, keep it somewhere where you can see it or access it regularly. Set alarms on your phone or put it on your calendar like an appointment. But remember, this is not something that is set in stone. You might find that you need to make alterations to your reparenting plan shortly after getting started. This is because this is all new! So remember to be kind to yourself and allow for flexibility. Maybe you bit off more than you can chew and need to scale back on frequency. Maybe you can only do it once a month but you realize you need to set aside the better part of a whole day to spend time with your wounded inner children. Maybe you tried one of the exercises and it did not resonate with you so you need to change up your reparenting method. There are going to be things that do not work or "go wrong" in the beginning. That is not a bad thing. That is data for you to use to make adjustments. This itself is part of reparenting, as you are using active listening and self-awareness to honor the needs of your WICs and yourself, and practicing self-love by adjusting to meet those needs.

If this feels overwhelming, just remember to focus on the step in front of you. Ask yourself, *What is the next step I need to take?* You are not doing all of this work at once and there is no time limit. We sometimes want to "get it over with" when it comes to reparenting, but at its core, reparenting your wounded inner children is about creating a healthy relationship between you and you. It is about becoming a more self-aware, compassionate, and kinder person, to yourself and to your WICs. It is about healing the wounds of the past and reducing the symptoms of your now so that your future is full of the relief, peace, safety, and inner contentment you deserve. If, at any point, you feel confused or overwhelmed, come back to this truth. If your focus is to learn to listen better to those inner voices, to respond in kind, and to just *try*—that is enough and you will see progress and change.

Dan's Story

Dan sought counseling after his wife threatened to leave him for being an absent father and husband. As a husband he acted like a child, expecting his partner to do everything. As a father, he acted like his father, emotionally unavailable, harsh, and reactive. The shock of his wife's declaration left him desperate for answers. However, Dan was completely resistant to any sort of reparenting techniques and did not believe in WICs. So for the first year, Dan worked on increasing his self-awareness, educating himself about effective parenting habits, and disciplining himself to carry his fair share of the household tasks. During this time Dan became aware of "roadblocks" he seemed to encounter that were not from wounds or weaknesses. He did some digging into his childhood and discovered that he had been diagnosed with severe ADHD, but was never treated. This ripped open a whole can of worms.

Dan felt betrayed by his parents and overwhelming grief at how much easier his life could have been had he been given the help and support he needed. Dan prioritized treating his ADHD and connected with a doctor, a medication manager, and an occupational therapist to help him operate at his best. This shift in priorities dramatically changed his life. He processed through his emotions in session and practiced adopting a newer, kinder form of self-talk since he now understood he wasn't "just dumb and lazy." Dan's anxiety decreased, his self-esteem increased, his marriage improved, and his connection with his children deepened. One day Dan said, "I'm so glad I didn't let you take me down the path of all that reparenting nonsense. I would still be chasing my tail and crying about things I cannot change." I choked back a chuckle and Dan looked at me quizzically. "But don't you see?" I asked Dan. "You have been reparenting yourself this whole time…"

Chapter 12 Takeaways

- Reparenting your wounded inner children births a new lifestyle—one born of self-compassion, awareness, patience, and love.

- It takes time, intentionality, and dedication to reparent your WICs. Scheduling reparenting time on your calendar and being consistent will help you to see progress and feel relief more quickly.

- Creating a reparenting plan helps create the structure and accountability you need to prioritize yourself and your healing amidst your busy schedule.

Questions to Consider

- How much time are you going to set aside, and how often, to begin your reparenting your WICs?

- Fill out your reparenting plan and then reflect on it. Look at how much progress you have already made in terms of self-awareness, acknowledgment, and dedication to your own healing. What aspect of this journey are you most proud of so far?

- In what ways do you realize you have already started reparenting yourself and your wounded inner children? Write down every instance you can think of for both you and the WICs you have identified.

Growing Up

SECTION 4

CHAPTER 13

Temper Tantrums: Setbacks, Symptoms, and Self-Compassion

You have acquired the foundational knowledge regarding your wounded inner children and the tools necessary for reparenting them. All that is left is to, well, *actually* do the work. This is a defining moment for many people. You are at a crossroads in your healing journey. Will you go left? Down the well-known, well-worn path that consists of more of the same and eventually leads you back to this point. Or will you go right? Down the unknown and untraversed path that consists of challenges, changes, healing, and growth. We all *say* we want to go right, but most of us do not. Our wounds and fears, while painful, are familiar and comfortable. And our brains like comfortable. But our souls? Our souls seek freedom. We yearn for change and breakthrough but fail to recognize it lies at the end of that dark and twisty path. This is your opportunity to intentionally choose to go right. To break the cycle. To go down the unfamiliar path. No one says it better than Robert Frost in his poem "The Road Not Taken":

> "Two roads diverged in a wood, and I—I took the one less traveled by, And that has made all the difference."

It is time for things to be different. If you have read more self-help books than you can count, have a hundred half-finished workbooks, or have done the on-again, off-again counseling thing—this is your moment to make a change. You can do it because you are not alone. Many have gone before you, and a multitude of people are alongside you, on their own paths. One of the scariest aspects of choosing something different is the unknown. Sometimes not knowing what to expect or feeling powerless to prepare ourselves can be so terrifying that we are paralyzed to take action no matter how badly we want to experience healing. That is what this chapter is for. We are going to look at pitfalls and problems that we might encounter and prepare ourselves as best we can so that, hopefully, it feels less daunting and you find the courage to keep going.

Setbacks

In the reparenting journey, you will have setbacks. You will push too hard and need to take a break to recoup. You will tire and need to rest. You will be emotionally and mentally sore. You will have days that you just do *not* want to do it. Like with any other healthy habit we want to incorporate into our lives, it is a process, and often a messy one. We are not aiming for "perfection"; we are aiming for progress. Progress that occurs over time and at a pace you feel comfortable with. There is a progress report worksheet for you to use in the free materials. Remember, some of your wounded inner children have been unknown, ignored, or neglected for years. Some of your wounds were formed over decades. Some of the beliefs you hold about yourself started at birth. It is going to take time to connect with, heal, and reparent these parts of yourself. Anything that takes time is going to encounter setbacks. Reparenting is no different. When we learn about a new method of healing it can ignite hope within us. That hope creates motivation, and that motivation will last right up until we slam into our first setback. It is at that moment that most people quit and turn back. Those who can get back up and keep going have a plan for their setbacks because they anticipate them. So what are your setbacks going to be? Take a moment to reflect on times in your life (without judgment) that you have quit after a setback. What happened? Why? Is it the same setbacks that get you every time? Get clear on what they are. Here are the most common ones that tend to come up to help get you thinking:

- Life is busy and we struggle to prioritize reparenting ourselves.

- Bumping into a wound or a memory we are not ready to deal with.

- Having current relationships with the people who wounded us and being scared of how healing might impact our relationship with them.

- Having questions about the process and feeling too scared to ask.

- Not seeing the progress we are making.

Have a plan for how you are going to handle your setbacks so that they do not derail you. HINT: Your plan can*not* be to "just keep going." White knuckling our healing does not get us anywhere. Your plan should be rooted in self-compassion and something that will encourage you to keep going. It can include things like:

- Creating a realistic schedule that you can sustain and adjusting as needed.

- Writing down that wound or memory and sealing it in an envelope until you feel ready to deal with it.

- Remembering that this is an internal journey, and you are not obligated to address anything with anyone.

- Ask the question. Reach out to me. Reach out to a professional. Use the free resources. Do not let a question or confusion stop you.

- Look for the little things and celebrate them big time. Did you think about *maybe* wanting to try one of the reparenting exercises sometime soon? That is huge! Pat yourself on the back!

Setbacks are part of the process. They are not reflective of your efforts and they do not mean that you have failed. Our biggest breakthroughs can come from bumping into a setback and simply committing to figuring it out. Our WICs see that we are willing to do whatever it takes to help them heal, we show ourselves love and care, and we become empowered and emboldened to keep going when we break through. Accept that setbacks will happen and commit to continuing on because you deserve healing.

Symptoms

Remember all those pesky symptoms we talked about in chapter 4? Sometimes they can pop back up (if they have been dormant) or intensify a bit when we are in the throes of reparenting. This is largely due to our brains simply trying to protect us. Imagine you got burned touching a stovetop. Your brain does not want you to touch it ever again, because *ow*. But you see that the stove is still on, so you reach out to turn it off. All your brain sees is you are reaching for the same thing that hurt you so it starts freaking out. That "freaking out" often manifests as anxiety, a trauma response, or even just plain ol' fear. Your brain is just trying to keep you safe, not understanding your intentions. Our brains can sometimes struggle to recognize when we are remembering something and not reliving it. As we allow our WICs to show us experiences that hurt us, or connect with emotions that need to be felt so that they can be dealt with, our brain might feel like it is happening again and respond in kind. This is where the use of professional support can come in handy. Mental health professionals are safe people who create safe spaces so that you can work through your wounds without retraumatizing yourself. Reparenting work is some of the deepest healing we do, so professional support is always recommended. However, if that is not a path you can or do not want to take, work this checklist before beginning your reparenting journey:

- Have at least one safe person you can reach out to as needed who knows you are reparenting.

- Fill your mental health toolbox with grounding exercises and regulation techniques.

- Understand your distress tolerance levels. How much discomfort, mentally or emotionally, can you handle without having a trauma response? Work to increase your distress tolerance and stay within your threshold when doing any reparenting work.

- Have a plan for if you bump into a wound, memory, or symptom that feels too big for you to handle on your own. There are amazing therapeutic communities, support groups, and resources out there.

Having a solid self-care routine is vital to managing any symptom increase. No, this is not just bubble baths and manicures. Self-care is an intentional plan to take care of you and your WICs *beforehand* and on an *ongoing basis*. Too many people are doing aftercare and calling it self-care. For example, self-care is knowing when to take a break and have some fun. If you are a parent you know that taking a break, having some fun, or being silly is just as much a part of parenting as the rest of it. The same is true of reparenting. This is not a race; your wounds will not heal faster by pushing yourself. The point of reparenting is to create a connection with your WICs born of safety and love. Skipping rocks in the river, buying a cake and having it for dinner, or dancing in your living room *is* reparenting and great self-care. So ask yourself, *What brings me relief and recharges my batteries mentally, emotionally, physically, and socially?*

Regression

Regression is a very real and very interesting phenomenon. Originally introduced by Freud, regression is when a person essentially "retreats"—mentally, emotionally, or behaviorally—to an earlier stage of development (Lokko and Stern 2015). A common example of regression is when older children regress in their speech and talk like a baby, often called "baby talk." A child's regression into baby talk can happen for a myriad of reasons, such as the birth of a sibling or a major disruption in life like divorce or a family move. However, regression happens with adults as well. Particularly adults with childhood trauma. Regression can be triggered by distress, fear, insecurity, or anger. We often regress in an attempt to retreat to an earlier time where we might have felt safe, innocent, or had someone who protected us. Regression exists on a spectrum and can range from subtle and harmless (wanting to snuggle with a stuffed animal) to more overt and harmful (having a temper tantrum that involves lashing out). While not exceedingly prevalent, when reparenting your WICs, you may encounter regression at times. If your childhood trauma was extreme and you are concerned about regression, I encourage you to seek professional guidance and support. However, for many of us, regression may be a way that your WIC is trying to express itself or get your attention. It could look like:

- Feeling vulnerable, small, needy, or scared in the ways a child would

- Feeling overwhelmed with emotion and a desire to express it in childlike ways (such as sobbing uncontrollably, wanting to throw a fit, rocking back and forth)

- Feeling as if you are younger internally ("I feel like I'm six years old again.")
- Developing interests in more childlike things (movies, hobbies, toys, or games)

All of these, and however else you may experience regression, are okay. All behavior is communication of an unmet need. So if you find your behavior feeling childlike, ask yourself, *What is it that I (or my WIC) need at this moment?* Just like with children, we often are needing comfort, reassurance, or to be heard and validated. Hugging yourself, creating safety, or allowing yourself to cry are small gestures, but powerful ones that often soothe our WICs in the same manner they would soothe an actual child. Try them and any other compassionate responses out to see what works best for you! Remember that recognizing how you are feeling, asking what your WIC needs, and working to meet that need are all forms of reparenting that will bring healing!

Paige's Story

Paige was excited to *finally* deal with the wounds that hurt her and the past that plagued her. She eagerly signed up for my Reparenting Your Inner Child workshop, attended every session, took ample notes, and asked lots of questions. Three weeks after the workshop concluded, Paige reached out saying that she was frustrated, felt stuck, and didn't know what to do. She had created a daily schedule of affirmations and was setting aside time twice a week to practice reparenting, but she did not think it was working. She felt worse. She felt exhausted, was crying all the time, and was having nightmares. She said she must "clearly be doing it wrong" because she was not better. I asked her why she was doing so much so soon and what the rush was. She clapped back saying, "Because I don't want to feel this way anymore! I have been feeling this way all my life and nothing makes it go away!" I asked Paige if maybe what her WIC needed was not to be rushed to be better, but instead to just be heard and validated. Paige had an ahha moment. She was *still* treating her WIC like her mom had treated her. Like a burden whose emotions were an inconvenience. Paige realized that her symptoms were her WIC pushing against the perpetuated neglect and crying out to be heard. Paige decided right then that her new plan was to just cry if she needed to cry, to listen and validate her WIC, and to prioritize rest. A month later Paige reached out saying she not only felt better than she had in years (the nightmares and exhaustion were gone), but that she had cried more in one month than she had in ten years—and it felt great! Her new "reparenting plan" was to learn how to play and have fun in life, something she never got to do before.

Chapter 13 Takeaways

- The reparenting journey involves setbacks, so plan for them and do not let them deter you.

- Symptoms can sometimes increase as we are reparenting our WICs. That is okay. Have a plan and do not hesitate to seek professional help if you feel that is necessary.

- Regression can sometimes occur when dealing with childhood wounds; approach it from a place of curiosity, not self-judgment. Use professional support if needed.

Questions to Consider

- What are my most likely setbacks going to be? What is my plan for handling them?

- What symptoms (if any) am I concerned about experiencing? What is my plan for dealing with them?

- Do I feel the use of professional support would be beneficial or necessary? If so, what is one step I can take to move toward getting the support I need?

CHAPTER 14

The Impact: Healed Inner Children Help Heal the World

While this book may be coming to a close, your healing is just beginning. This book was not intended to contain the entirety of your reparenting journey, but rather to introduce you to it. You may feel uncomfortable or unsure of your next steps, but that is not only okay, it is a good thing. We live in a day and age of wanting things clear cut, spelled out, formulated, and immediate. Unfortunately, reparenting your wounded inner child (or children) is none of those things. But that is also what makes it so beautiful. It is messy, murky, sometimes confusing, and fiercely personal. This book was designed to equip you with the knowledge, language, and tools to increase your ability to be reflective and self-aware. But traversing down the path to reparenting yourself is up to you and something that you do on your own. However, you are not alone. While each reparenting journey is individualistic, we are all on this healing journey together. The question you are now facing and need to answer is: do I trust myself enough to take the next step?

You do not need to have it all figured out, and if you feel that you should, practice accepting the truth that you never will, and that is okay. There are WICs you are not aware of yet and wounds you are not ready to heal. If that feels scary or you feel like you *need* to know everything right now, practice accepting the truth that we never know it all, and that is okay. Life has a funny way of revealing to you what it is you are ready to heal. So pay attention to what is on your mind, what is happening in your life, and how you are feeling. You can use the prompts, exercises, and tools to give yourself some structure or guidance but you must recognize this important truth: reparenting your wounded inner children is something that is happening in your day-to-day moments. It is woven into the way you speak to yourself, the thoughts you think, and those 10,000 small decisions you make every day. It is not just a workbook to complete or a course to pass and then you are done. It is a relationship with yourself. It is a healing journey that takes you from your place of woundedness to a place of wholeness.

The most important ingredients to reparenting are self-compassion, kindness, and love. All the exercises and affirmations mean nothing if you are not practicing these three things. That is because self-compassion, kindness, and love are what your wounded inner children need most. Every traumatic experience or hurtful moment your WICs experienced had at least one of those ingredients lacking. So if *all* you do is find ways in which you can practice being a little more compassionate toward yourself, that will bring about profound healing and change. While that sounds simple and somewhat counterintuitive (we expect big wounds to require big action), when you think about actually living from a place of self-compassion, it can feel overwhelming and sometimes impossible. But remember—from the moment you picked up this book, you have been practicing self-compassion. With every "ahha," every highlighted sentence or underlined paragraph, with every tear that has fallen or curse word you have dropped, you have been increasing your self-compassion. You have been learning to love yourself a little bit more. Every memory you recalled, every trauma you validated, every WIC you have acknowledged, you have been making the shift from blindly judging yourself and feeling shame to gaining insight and understanding. That shift slathers your wounds in the soothing balm of self-compassion, allowing them to begin healing. You have begun healing.

As you practice the reparenting exercises and incorporate the tools into your daily living, you will find yourself gaining confidence and momentum. The more you allow the process to be messy, to have stops and starts, the easier it will be to keep moving forward. Remember, practice makes progress, not perfection. The concept of perfection is often just one of your wounded inner children seeking acceptance. You are in the process of learning a new language, a new way of treating yourself, and a new perspective toward your past. So be patient with yourself and recognize that it takes time to reparent your wounded inner children. Rushing the process or quitting will not make it go any faster. Your wounds are not going anywhere anyway, so you can take all the time you need and go at the pace you are most comfortable with. The goal is the journey itself. To just keep going. To not quit, to keep trying, to keep healing is one of the greatest most radical acts of self-love we can do.

The Impact of Reparenting

Reparenting your wounded inner children does not just help you live a better life; it has a ripple effect that touches the lives of everyone you know. When we can be compassionate with ourselves, we are often able to be more compassionate with others who reflect back to us the behaviors we judged in ourselves. When we understand why we act the way we do without judgment, we can more clearly see the wounds that drive the actions of those around us. Living a life of authenticity, self-acceptance, and love provides an example to those around you. Every human on this planet has experienced being wounded and wanting relief from the pain of that wound—whether physical, mental, or emotional. The best thing you could ever do to help others is to heal yourself. In doing so you showcase what is possible, and that gives people hope. Hope that change, relief, and peace are possible is what causes us to keep going, to keep trying.

One of the greatest outcomes of reparenting is that it protects future generations from generational trauma and abuse by breaking the cycle. If you are a parent you might have experienced that pang of desperation for your children to be protected or spared from the hurt and pain you have known. The desire for our children to have a better experience is what has driven the evolution of humanity. We live in a day and age of instant access to information, which has made us acutely aware of the tragedies and horrors that exist. However, research is clear that we are healthier than ever and living in safer times than at any other time in the history of humanity (Gentry 2022).

Trauma (what it is and what causes it) is increasingly becoming common knowledge. Our awareness of what abuse looks like and the impact it has on us is more clearly understood than ever before. Accessing services like therapy; attending support groups, workshops, and seminars; and reading self-help books are less stigmatized and becoming normalized. Younger generations, particularly millennials, are seeking education and guidance on how to be the best parents they can be and *not* perpetuate toxic family cycles. All of this is helping improve us as the human race. But the thing that holds the greatest impact has always been and always will be one's own personal healing. Imagine if your caregivers had done the work. What would have been different for you? What if your grandparents or great-grandparents had done the work? How would that have changed things? What experiences would you have had or not had? What wounds would not exist? Who would you be? How might you feel differently about yourself, others, and life in general?

The weight of breaking generational cycles and the balancing act of reparenting your wounded inner children while trying to parent your own children can feel heavy and daunting. Sometimes we have grief, resentment, or anger that we need to process through. But it is also one of the greatest honors that can be bestowed upon us. Your children and future generations will point at you and say, "It was because of the work they did that I am who I am today." If you desire to be a better parent, it starts with reparenting yourself. As hard as the work might be, it is work you will never regret doing. If you are younger or do not have children, there is no better time to do this work. The sooner you prioritize your reparenting journey the quicker you take your power back. Trauma, abuse, and the painful memories of your past have stolen enough from your life. Do not let them steal another second. If you are older, maybe your children are already raised, understand that it is not too late. Sometimes we have grief that we did not learn something sooner, and that is okay. But celebrate that you are here now and that you deserve to put down the hurt and pain you have been carrying for far too long and experience the relief and peace that is rightfully yours.

The bottom line is—I believe in you, I am here to support you, and you are not alone. You can do this, you deserve this, and it is time to heal. Your wounded inner children are waiting for you...so let the reparenting begin!

My Story

The first person I ever walked through the reparenting journey was myself. In fact, my reparenting journey continues today. Two days before I wrote the final chapter of this book, I stumbled upon a WIC I did not know existed when I was suddenly, out of nowhere, slammed with intrusive, irrational thoughts regarding my own son. At the moment I did not understand what was happening. I was not aware my current circumstances had triggered a WIC within me who began crying out for help. And I certainly was not consciously thinking, *Oh look at this WIC I found, here let me reparent myself real quick for healing.* Quite the opposite. I was a hot mess of confusion, fear, pain, and panic. However, I have been on the reparenting journey long enough that I recognized those feelings and sensations as the clues they were. Something was happening inside of me.

I stuck to basics. I breathed. I recognized the urge to shove down the feelings and ignore the sensations I was experiencing in my body. And then I made the conscious choice to not act on that impulse. Instead, I opened my mouth, spoke up, and asked a friend to help me. I followed the impulses I was having (still unaware they were was the prompting of my new and unidentified wounded inner child). I allowed myself to express emotions I was feeling that I did not understand and felt embarrassed for having. I practiced being compassionate and gentle with myself. I asked myself, *What is my next step? What do I need to do to feel safe?* And when it all clicked and I realized what was happening, I seized the opportunity to reparent despite it being "inconvenient" timing. I gave my WIC permission to feel and say all the things she needed to. And boy did she have a lot to say. I held space for her. I cried with her. I validated her hurt and pain. I told her she deserved better and that I was sorry for what she went through. I promised her she was safe with me and that I would never treat her the way she had been treated. I hugged myself and swayed until I felt myself calm down, and my WIC breathed a sigh of relief. I journaled about what happened. I cried some more. Then I made myself a giant bowl of ice cream and threw a "slumber party" for me and my WIC. I slept the best I had in years that night.

My reparenting journey continues just like everyone else's. It is messy, twisty, and ever evolving. It is not a box to check or a goal to accomplish.

It is a way of living, a way of being.

It is giving ourselves a better ending than the beginning we had.

It is breaking the cycles of old and making way for the new.

It is a way of leaving this world just a little bit better than how we found it.

It is embodying the safe place we always longed for as children.

It is loving ourselves in the way we have always deserved.

Chapter 14 Takeaways

- Reparenting your wounded inner child, or children, is a way of living.

- Self-compassion, kindness, and love are the most important aspects of reparenting.

- This may be the end of the book, but it is just the beginning of your reparenting journey!

Questions to Consider

- What are five benefits (for myself and others) that I can identify from reparenting myself?

- What is one way I can practice being compassionate to myself today?

- What is my next step?

Acknowledgments

First and foremost, thank you to New Harbinger Publications and my editor Jennye Garibaldi. You took a chance on me that changed my life. You were long suffering and incredibly patient as I stumbled my way through this process. You were supportive and encouraging every step of the way. I would not have acknowledgments to write if it were not for you. I cannot begin to convey the depths of my gratitude to you.

To Dr. Lindsay Gibson—I only ever had a chance with New Harbinger Publications because of you. You came into my life unexpectedly and our serendipitous connection will forever be one of the best things that has ever happened to me. Your guidance, mentoring, support, cheerleading, and kindness have been deeply healing for me. Your words of encouragement were a life vest for me when the writing waters got overwhelming. You are an inspiration, an incredible example, and an angel on this earth. My gratitude for you knows no bounds.

Thank you to Will and Mychele of the Academy of Self Help (ASH). In the domino effect that led me to this book, you were the first piece to fall into place. You found me on social media and invited me into your beautiful community. You were the ones who introduced me to Dr. Gibson. You were the ones who fanned my flame, gave me a platform, and created a safe space for me to grow as a professional and a person. I owe so much to you.

To my tripod of support: Mary Mathis-Burnett, Andria Downes, and Michael Downes. You are my best friends and my family. You were also the wall I beat myself against when I feared I could not do it and the safe space I collapsed into when I did. You dealt with all my freak-outs, managed all my meltdowns, spurred me on when I wanted to quit, and forced me to celebrate myself. I love you three fiercely.

Thank you to my family. My mother April, my father Michael, and my brother and sister-in-law Charlie and Jamie. Mom and Dad, you fanned the flame of my passion for writing since childhood and always said I would be an author. Thank you for always believing in me. Charlie and Jamie, your encouragement, enthusiasm, and support kept me going when I doubted myself. I am so grateful to all of you.

To my clients—you guys are the real heroes here. Thank you for trusting me with your stories, your wounded inner children, your hearts, and your healing journeys. Thank you for allowing me to share your experiences with the world so that others can have hope. Thank you for never quitting on yourselves, for believing in yourselves, and for knowing you deserve healing and freedom. Walking alongside you on your repainting journeys has been the greatest professional honor of my life.

Lastly, thank you to my son. Your entrance into my life kicked off my reparenting journey. My love for you gave me the courage to face my deepest fears and darkest demons. I would not be the person I am today without you. You are the greatest thing I have ever, or will ever create. You brought joy into my life at levels I did not know were possible, and loving you taught me what real, true love is. My greatest endeavor in life is to give you a childhood you do not need to heal from. I love you forever and always.

References

American Psychiatric Association. 2022. *Diagnostic and Statistical Manual of Mental Disorders*. 5th ed., Text Revision. Arlington, VA: American Psychiatric Association.

Anderson, F. G. 2021. *Transcending Trauma: Healing Complex PTSD with Internal Family Systems*. Eau Claire, WI: PESI Publishing.

Basten, C., and S. Touyz. 2020. "Sense of Self: Its Place in Personality Disturbance, Psychopathology, and Normal Experience." *Review of General Psychology* 24(2): 159–171. https://doi.org/10.1177/1089268019880884.

Baumrind, D. 1971. "Current Patterns of Parental Authority." *Developmental Psychology* 4: 1–103. https://doi.org/10.1037/h0030372.

Berne, E. 1989. *Transactional Analysis in Psychotherapy: A Systematic Individual and Social Psychiatry*. New York: Ballantine Books.

Brown, Brené. 2010. *The Gifts of Imperfection*. Minneapolis, MN: Hazelden Publishing.

Brown, E. J., A. Cohen, A. P. Mannarino. 2020. "Trauma-Focused Cognitive-Behavioral Therapy: The Role of Caregivers." *Journal of Affective Disorders* 277: 39–45.

Capacchione, L. 1991. *Recovery of Your Inner Child*. New York: Simon and Schuster.

Erikson, E. H. 1950. *Childhood and Society*. New York: W. W. Norton and Company.

Erikson, E. H. 1994. *Identity and the Life Cycle*. New York: W. W. Norton and Company.

Fox, E. 1960. *The Wonder Child*. Camarillo, CA: DeVorss Publications.

Frost, R. 1968. *Complete Poems of Robert Frost*. Austin, TX: Holt, Rinehart and Winston.

Gentry, J. E. 2022. *Forward-Facing Trauma Therapy: Healing the Moral Wound*. 2nd ed. Parker, CO: Outskirts Press.

James, M. 1985. *Breaking Free: Self-Reparenting for a New Life.* San Francisco, CA: Addison-Wesley Publishing Company.

Janov, A. 1975. *The Feeling Child: Preventing Neurosis in Children.* New York: Simon and Schuster.

Jung, C. G., and C. Kerényi. 1951. *Introduction to a Science of Mythology: The Myth of the Divine Child and the Mysteries of Eleusis.* Translated by R. F. C. Hull. London: Routledge and Paul.

Kuppens, S., and E. Ceulemans. 2019. "Parenting Styles: A Closer Look at a Well-Known Concept." *Journal of Child and Family Studies* 28(1): 168–181. https://doi.org/10.1007/s10826-018-1242-x.

Lokko, H. N., and T. A. Stern. 2015. "Regression: Diagnosis, Evaluation, and Management." *The Primary Care Companion for CNS Disorders* 17(3). https://doi.org/10.4088/PCC.14f01761.

Mann, D. 2021. *Gestalt Therapy: 100 Key Points and Techniques.* London: Routledge Books.

Maté, G., and D. Maté. 2022. *The Myth of Normal: Trauma, Illness, and Healing in a Toxic Culture.* London: Penguin Random House.

Sanvictores T., M. D. Mendez. 2022. *Types of Parenting Styles and Effects on Children.* Treasure Island, FL: StatPearls Publishing.

Schiff, J. L., and B. D. Romulo. 1970. *All My Children.* New York: M. Evans.

Schwartz, R. C. 2021. *No Bad Parts: Healing Trauma and Restoring Wholeness.* London: Penguin Random House.

Schwartz, R. C. 2023. *Introduction to Internal Family Systems.* Boulder, CO: Sounds True.

Sharman, L. S., G. A. Dingle, M. Baker, A. Fischer, A. Gračanin, I. Kardum, and H. Manley et al. 2019. "The Relationship of Gender Roles and Beliefs to Crying in an International Sample." *Frontiers in Psychology* 10: 2288. https://doi.org/10.3389/fpsyg.2019.02288.

Van der Kolk, B. 2015. *The Body Keeps the Score: Brain, Mind, and Body in the Healing of Trauma.* New York: Penguin Books.

Watts, J. R., N. R. Lazzareschi, Y. Liu, and D. O'Sullivan. 2023. "Childhood Psychological Maltreatment, Sense of Self, and PTSD Symptoms in Emerging Adulthood." *Journal of Counseling and Development* 101(1): 96–105. https://doi.org/10.1002/jcad.12455.

Whitfield, C. L. 2006. *Healing the Child Within: Discovery and Recovery for Adult Children of Dysfunctional Families.* Deerfield, FL: Health Communications.

Nicole Johnson, LPC, MEd, is a licensed professional counselor and certified clinical trauma professional with a dual master's in education and counseling, and a bachelor's degree in political science. A member of the American Counseling Association and the International Society for Traumatic Stress Studies, Johnson is also a certified life coach, and is owner and founder of Oak and Ivy Therapy Services. She is known as "The Ginger Shrink" on social media, and offers her nationally available virtual psychoeducation course on trauma and abuse called "Get a G.R.I.P." Johnson presents at conferences around the country where she frequently speaks on childhood trauma, abuse, and her unique approach to healing. She hosts a virtual workshop on "Reparenting Your Inner Child," and lives in Boise, ID. You can find out more about Johnson at www.thegingershrink.squarespace.com.

Foreword writer **Lindsay C. Gibson, PsyD**, is a clinical psychologist and psychotherapist with more than thirty years' experience working in both public service and private practice. Her books—including the *New York Times* bestseller, *Adult Children of Emotionally Immature Parents*—have sold more than a million copies, and have been translated into thirty-seven languages. In the past, Gibson has served as an adjunct assistant professor, teaching doctoral clinical psychology students clinical theory and psychotherapy techniques. Gibson lives and works in Virginia Beach, VA.

Real change *is* possible

For more than fifty years, New Harbinger has published proven-effective self-help books and pioneering workbooks to help readers of all ages and backgrounds improve mental health and well-being, and achieve lasting personal growth. In addition, our spirituality books offer profound guidance for deepening awareness and cultivating healing, self-discovery, and fulfillment.

Founded by psychologist Matthew McKay and Patrick Fanning, New Harbinger is proud to be an independent, employee-owned company. Our books reflect our core values of integrity, innovation, commitment, sustainability, compassion, and trust. Written by leaders in the field and recommended by therapists worldwide, New Harbinger books are practical, accessible, and provide real tools for real change.

MORE BOOKS from NEW HARBINGER PUBLICATIONS

ADULT CHILDREN OF EMOTIONALLY IMMATURE PARENTS

How to Heal from Distant, Rejecting, or Self-Involved Parents

978-1626251700 / US $18.95

ADULT SURVIVORS OF TOXIC FAMILY MEMBERS

Tools to Maintain Boundaries, Deal with Criticism, and Heal from Shame After Ties Have Been Cut

978-1684039289 / US $19.95

HEALING RELATIONAL TRAUMA

Move Beyond Painful Childhood Experiences to Deepen Self-Understanding and Build Authentic Relationships

978-1648484384 / US $19.95

THE POLYVAGAL SOLUTION

Vagus Nerve-Calming Practices to Soothe Stress, Ease Emotional Overwhelm, and Build Resilience

978-1648484124 / US $19.95

THE SELF-COMPASSION DAILY JOURNAL

Let Go of Your Inner Critic and Embrace Who You Are with Acceptance and Commitment Therapy

978-1648482496 / US $18.95

THE UNTETHERED SOUL

The Journey Beyond Yourself

978-1572245372 / US $18.95

newharbingerpublications

1-800-748-6273 / newharbinger.com

(VISA, MC, AMEX / prices subject to change without notice)

Follow Us

Don't miss out on new books from New Harbinger.
Subscribe to our email list at **newharbinger.com/subscribe**